'In *Sublimation and Superego*, Jared Russell opens up a transitional space where Freud is brought into conversation with Sophocles, Heidegger, Nietzsche and Deleuze as well as post-Freudian psychoanalysts like Loewald and Bollas. In this space, the dialogue between these thinkers transcends the disciplinary boundaries of ontology, metaphysics, psychoanalysis and deconstruction. *Sublimation and Superego* points the way to a deeper understanding of the relationship between self and other, both in and out of the clinic.'

Mikita Brottman, *Maryland Institute College of Art, USA*

'A timely retrieval of the question of sublimation for psychoanalysis. The third installment of an author whose rigorous sincerity shows the great value of clinicians and theorists responding to the critical discoveries of Nietzsche.'

Tim Themi, *University of Melbourne, Australia*

Sublimation and Superego

This book integrates a thinking about dilemmas faced in the context of the clinical practice of psychoanalysis today, with contemporary social and political concerns specific to the age of the global consumer marketplace.

Beginning with an analysis of the fate of the concept of sublimation in Freud's work, and its relationship to the elaboration of the concept of the superego in 1923, Jared Russell examines how these concepts provide a lever for integrating psychoanalytic thinking with topics of urgent social concern, beyond the critique of ideology. Taking up topics such as the experience of time, addiction to consumption, and the general consequences of the insinuation of digital technologies at increasingly earlier stages in human development—and thinking these through the lens of what the clinical practice of psychoanalysis teaches us about intimate human relatedness—the book addresses how a philosophically oriented approach to psychoanalysis can illuminate our response to the problems of everyday life under conditions of late capitalism. Drawing on a diverse range of authors such as Freud, Heidegger, Hans Loewald, Christopher Bollas, Lacan, Deleuze and Bernard Stiegler, it is argued that the concepts of sublimation and of the superego must be reinvented with regard to both clinical and critical discourse today if psychoanalysis is to remain relevant to the major issues we face, both individually and collectively, in the twenty-first century.

Sublimation and Superego: Psychoanalysis Between Two Deaths stages a unique encounter between philosophy, critical theory and clinical practice that will be of interest to psychoanalysts, scholars of twentieth-century continental philosophy, critical social theorists and mental health practitioners.

Jared Russell, PhD, is a psychoanalyst in private practice in New York City. He is the author of *Nietzsche and the Clinic: Psychoanalysis, Philosophy, Metaphysics* (Routledge 2017) and *Psychoanalysis and Deconstruction: Freud's Psychic Apparatus* (Routledge 2020).

Sublimation and Superego

Psychoanalysis Between Two Deaths

Jared Russell

Cover credit: © Ganesh Shivaswmay Foundation

First published 2022
by Routledge
4 Park Square, Milton Park, Abingdon, Oxon OX14 4RN

and by Routledge
605 Third Avenue, New York, NY 10158

Routledge is an imprint of the Taylor & Francis Group, an informa business

© 2022 Jared Russell

The right of Jared Russell to be identified as author of this work has been asserted in accordance with sections 77 and 78 of the Copyright, Designs and Patents Act 1988.

All rights reserved. No part of this book may be reprinted or reproduced or utilised in any form or by any electronic, mechanical, or other means, now known or hereafter invented, including photocopying and recording, or in any information storage or retrieval system, without permission in writing from the publishers.

Trademark notice: Product or corporate names may be trademarks or registered trademarks, and are used only for identification and explanation without intent to infringe.

British Library Cataloguing-in-Publication Data
A catalogue record for this book is available from the British Library

Library of Congress Cataloging-in-Publication Data
Names: Russell, Jared, author.
Title: Sublimation and superego : psychoanalysis between two deaths / Jared Russell.
Description: New York, NY : Routledge, 2022. | Includes bibliographical references and index. | Identifiers: LCCN 2021030015 (print) | LCCN 2021030016 (ebook) | ISBN 9781032153803 (paperback) | ISBN 9781032153827 (hardback) | ISBN 9781003243878 (ebook)
Subjects: LCSH: Sublimation (Psychology) | Superego. | Critical theory. | Psychoanalysis.
Classification: LCC BF175.5.S92 R87 2022 (print) | LCC BF175.5.S92 (ebook) | DDC 150.19/5--dc23
LC record available at https://lccn.loc.gov/2021030015
LC ebook record available at https://lccn.loc.gov/2021030016

ISBN: 978-1-032-15382-7 (hbk)
ISBN: 978-1-032-15380-3 (pbk)
ISBN: 978-1-003-24387-8 (ebk)

DOI: 10.4324/9781003243878

Typeset in Bembo
by MPS Limited, Dehradun

For Ashley Lambert

Contents

	Acknowledgments	x
	Introduction	1
1	Freud—sublimation and superego	9
2	Hans Loewald—between Freud and Heidegger	35
3	The fundamental ontology of Christopher Bollas	60
4	*Antigone*—sublimation as transgressive autonomy	79
5	Weapons	100
	Index	129

Acknowledgments

For their support during the writing of this project, I would like to thank my friends and colleagues Yukari Yanagino, Das Aniti, Alan Bass, Stefan Petraske, Andy Ritzo, Ryan Keagan, Sam Luebke, Melissa Daum and Andra Grants. As always, Rebecca Wallance was invaluable in helping to prepare the final manuscript. Special thanks to Doug Stanhope, who is the voice of my generation.

Sections of Chapter 5 were previously published in "Sick of It All," *The Agonist: A Nietzsche Circle Journal*, special issue on Nietzsche and Illness (2021). Epigraph to Chapter 5 from *Venom and Honey*, by Jayalalita devi dasi (2016), used with kind permission granted by the author and Martinet Press.

Introduction

In *The Future of an Illusion*, Freud (1927) writes,

> It is not true that the human mind has undergone no development since the earliest times and that, in contrast to the advances in science and technology, it is the same today as it was at the beginning of history. (p. 190)

He goes on to cite the emergence of the superego as evidence of the fact that our biological inheritance has been modified by historical influences. Ever wary of (though often succumbing to) biological reductionism, Freud insistently argued that human beings have not always experienced their world in some fundamentally immutable way, that the general framework in which human beings relate themselves to an external world is possessed of its own evolutionary dynamic, like the evolution of knowledge and of technology. What we call mind has not only an individual but a collective developmental history, and this history is subject to alteration and regression. Our individual minds are the effects of our collective history of interaction with our environment. For this reason, it is always possible for us to lose our minds, both individually and collectively. Psychoanalysis is a response to this threatening possibility.

Despite its theoretical standing in certain remote corners of academia usually associated with cultural studies, the clinical practice of psychoanalysis is in a state of crisis, and its future is more uncertain now than ever. In this way, the current state of the discipline reflects the state of our natural, social and political environments today. This parallel is not incidental. It is not simply the case that psychoanalysis is in a state of crisis due to its internal rivalries as a discipline, and due to the accelerating proliferation of alternative forms of psychological treatment—even those marketed under the advertising campaigns of the "evidence-based" and the "results-oriented." The wager of the present text is that psychoanalysis is in a state of crisis because those basic foundations of human psychological experience that once made analytic therapy effective are themselves massively and everywhere under siege today. That is, psychoanalysis is receding as a preferred form of mental health

DOI: 10.4324/9781003243878-101

2 *Introduction*

treatment because human beings themselves are undergoing profound changes at the psychological, neurological and sociocultural levels. These levels are irreducibly intertwined and cannot legitimately be considered divorced from one another, despite the ways in which the distribution of information about each has made it impossible to keep up with an understanding of their inherent integration. Human beings both influence and are products of their environment. Our contemporary environment is modifying human experience in ways that remain concealed to us. One of the sites where the traces of these modifications can be discerned is the psychoanalytic clinic and in the general decline of its perceived effectiveness.

Freud's work, both theoretical and clinical, was entirely based on the controversial assertion made by Jean-Martin Charcot that psychological illnesses, of which there are no discernible organic bases, are real. This remains as radical and controversial an assertion today as it was when it first appeared. Against the prevailing attitude—then as now—that non-organic, psychological suffering is simply "all in one's head," and is therefore most amenable to behavioral and chemical treatments, Charcot had insisted that purely psychological disorders (beginning with hysteria) are real, and that *the mind is capable of making itself sick, without recognizing that it is in the process of doing so*. Contained within this assertion was the insistence that the mind is not simply an epiphenomenon of neurological functioning, that while neurologically supported, the mind has its own independent existence and is capable of producing effects on the body and on matter more generally. Freud was well aware that this assertion can appear unscientific, in that it appears to invoke a substantial concept of mind which risks harkening back to the pre-scientific concept of the soul. But Freud fought his entire career to establish the scientificity of this claim, and of psychoanalysis as a body of knowledge and as a form of treatment rooted in this transformative understanding—an understanding that, Freud came to concede, and as is universally accepted among analysts today, cannot be transmitted theoretically but that must be experienced. This is the experience of the clinic.

A clinic of interpretation was based on the assumption that cultivating an understanding of self-experience would inherently facilitate change and could therefore serve as the basis for a properly therapeutic procedure. For decades, there seemed no reason to challenge this basic assumption, and psychoanalysis thrived in a culture where this was the case. More recently, repetitive symptomatic behaviors have become increasingly divorced from psychological experience, and the power to facilitate change by means of self-understanding is challenged at every moment by the oppression of the consumer marketplace. The symptom today appears structured according to the logic of addiction, and no longer treatable with the model of repression. However, it may not be the case that as a result, and as its critics insist, psychoanalysis "does not work," but the question as to *how* it might best work in relation to contemporary psychological and systemic disorders—how psychoanalysis might respond to a world that has become so overwhelmingly pathological that it actively pursues its own destruction, in ever-accelerating and increasingly uncontrollable ways—is a question that demands serious attention.

Analysts have long labored under the assumption that by cultivating their patients' defensively blocked but established capacities for symbolization they could induce therapeutic change. Today we face cultural, political and economic conditions that ruin the establishment of these capacities at their very bases. If psychoanalysis fails to produce "results" quickly enough to satisfy representatives of the insurance industry or those who consider psychotherapy a form of consumer effectiveness service, this is not because its claims about the mind are unsubstantiated but because the world in which we currently live is compelled to judge standards of "mental health" far differently than only a century ago.

Reinventing a clinic of interpretation today is thus not a question of abandoning Freud's insights in favor of a clinical approach that responds more immediately to contemporary cognitive styles. Psychoanalysis must rather reinvent itself as an effort to fight for the cultivation of symbolizing capacities that was previously at the heart of the civilizing process. Concrete, positivistic fact-mindedness—which is the *opposite* of the ability to appreciate critically and to assess facts—has become the new general strategy for managing psychological suffering, and in this way it is replacing the ability to symbolize self-experience which previously served the same end.[1] Minds saturated by digital overstimulation and by injunctions relentlessly to consume are in need of an interpretive approach now more than ever, but this requires that psychoanalysis reassess its conceptual bases and clinical procedures.

It is also on this basis that psychoanalysis must assert its *intrinsically* political orientation today. By this, I do not mean the relevance of psychoanalytic concepts for political theorizing, but the clinic as a site of resistance to the destructive politics of a pervasively spiritualized (financialized) marketplace. This destruction—both ecological and psychological, and in ways that reveal their interdetermination—brings this dimension of clinical practice into focus. The traditional practice of therapeutic interpretation had always grounded itself in the assumption that by liberating blocked passageways toward symbolization, this could lead to personal transformation. Again, there are no longer any such grounds for this assumption. Environmental conditions today are organized around ruining our ability to symbolize. The insinuation of digital technologies into the lives of increasingly younger potential consumer demographics creates a culture in which identification with primary caregivers, and the capacities for symbolization that emerge from such identifications, are insistently short-circuited and appropriated by marketing strategies designed to provide human beings with the objects of their desire before the *question* as to individual desire is even posed.

For this reason, efforts to reintroduce political theory into psychoanalysis or vice versa today entirely miss the point, continuing to situate themselves in a purely academic context. What needs to be thought is how psychoanalysis as an effort at cultivating the ability to symbolize and to sublimate functions as a

4   *Introduction*

form of resistance to the destruction of those abilities encouraged by the contemporary marketplace, which has entirely subsumed the place of culture, community and tradition. Nowhere in the present text is there an effort to inject a political perspective into contemporary psychoanalytic theory, or to think the political through an analytic lens. The critique of ideology is a trend whose time has passed—it is simply *too late* for that. Dire circumstances require instead that we grasp how the *work* of psychoanalysis as a clinical practice has become irreducibly radicalized by a purely speculative economy that now thrives on debasing individuals' abilities to think symbolically.

The vexed concept of sublimation in the psychoanalytic literature provides a lever for initiating this effort. Any literate professional working within the field will know that sublimation is a concept with a peculiar and complex history. How and why this has been the case will be the topic of my opening chapter. The ultimate intention of my argument is to demonstrate that sublimation has been a difficult concept for analysts (beginning with Freud himself) to assess because it challenges deeply rooted, classical prejudices about the ways in which we are to conceive of the relationship between mind and world.

Analysts have made the mistake of imagining sublimation to be among the various means by which human beings manage psychological experience (i.e., the defenses). I intend to argue, following Loewald (1988), that sublimation must rather be conceived as the *constitution* of psychological experience—as the process of *individuation* that occurs in that space *between* mind and world, and that both constitutes and is a product of the relation of *responsibility* that links self and environment. Sublimation involves not just the transformation of what Freud called "thing-presentations" (*Sachevorstellungen*) into "word-presentations" (*Wortvorstellungen*), but the ability to relate oneself to the ideals of the sociocultural field at large, and as these are intergenerationally transmitted. It is this ability more specifically that is everywhere subject to control and disposal in our current environment, resulting in immeasurable conditions of psychological suffering that are at once in excess, and in desperate need, of a psychoanalytic, interpretive approach.

According to the pre-Socratic philosopher Heraclitus, "The path up and down is one and the same" (Kirk, Raven and Schofield 1983, p. 188). At the origin of the Western tradition, this paradoxical insight was eclipsed by Platonic idealism and by Aristotelian rationalism which, consolidated into a singular vision that would come to be called humanism in the wake of the sixteenth century, would form the basis for the Western Secular Enlightenment. At the beginning of the twentieth century, and in the general context of this globalizing development, this was an insight briefly and unwittingly retrieved by psychoanalysts with regard to the concept of sublimation. The status of this concept and the encounter that it registers has functioned as a source of difficulty for the discipline ever since. Freudian psychoanalysis sought to provide a rational basis for understanding the irrational. It was inevitable that such a project would discover irrational elements intrinsic to its own efforts to think the irrational rationally, and that it would try to suppress these elements. The theory of sublimation in psychoanalysis—and by theory I mean both the concept and the dynamic history of its elaboration—is a privileged place where these elements, which are necessary opportunities for both scientific and democratic advancement, have continued to assert themselves.

The central argument of the present text is thus that in order to demonstrate its continued relevance in the twenty-first century, psychoanalysis must finally come to terms with the concept of sublimation, and with it, that of the superego. This pertains to the status of analysis both as a body of knowledge and as a therapeutic method. A clinic that could accommodate for a worked-out theory of sublimation would be one updated to address the emotional difficulties brought on by the present age. At the same time, it is by means of such an account that psychoanalysis can demonstrate its wider sociopolitical relevance where cognitive, behavioral and pharmaceutical approaches necessarily fail by remaining complicit with market forces intent on disrupting the development of all capacities for sublimation and for spontaneous investment in care, imagination and desire.

★★★

Chapter 1 performs a reading of Freud on the topic of sublimation, which is bound up in a certain development of Freud's thinking that will culminate in the theory of the superego. Sublimation and superego are—by means of a series of other crucial terms that Freud elaborates—inextricably interrelated. Beginning already with Freud, however, the superego has been thought almost exclusively as a moral, self-punitive psychical agency, and is today most often portrayed via Lacan as a "pure culture of the death instinct" (Freud 1923, p. 53). This was not all Freud had to say about the concept, and we will return to an examination of the "other side" of the superego (the ego ideal) that relates to sublimation by opening the self to a sense that there is a future worth making investments in or "cathecting."

Chapter 2 takes up the work of Hans Loewald, whose *Sublimation* (1988) is arguably the most significant treatment of the topic in the history of the discipline. In order to do justice to the sophistication of Loewald's thinking, a good amount of time will initially be spent outlining the basic conceptual matrix of Heidegger's *Being and Time* (1996). The influence of Heidegger's thinking on Loewald is profound—much more so than those who casually refer to Loewald's tutelage under Heidegger seem ready to appreciate. Although sublimation was not a concept that could ever have found a home in Heidegger's project, Loewald's thinking about sublimation—like everything else Loewald thought about, including the superego—is thoroughly saturated with a Heideggerian inflection. Grasping this will help us better to understand how and why these concepts can and must be re-articulated today.

Chapter 3 further extends the engagement with Heidegger's thinking into a dialogue with Christopher Bollas. Despite situating a notion of extreme

6   *Introduction*

creativity at the heart of his approach to psychoanalysis, sublimation and superego are not terms Bollas ever appears to have had much time for. In this, Bollas follows the path cut by Winnicott, and for the same reason: Neither Winnicott nor Bollas sees that, for Freud, the capacity for sublimation has *everything* to do with the question of the impact of the developmental environment. The proximity of Heidegger and Bollas in certain regards—beyond Bollas's casual use of terms like "existential" and others that belong to the history of Heideggerian thought, while acknowledging that on closer scrutiny the deployment of these terms seems more deeply informed as to their meaning than on the surface appears to be the case—not only will allow us to integrate a revised thinking about sublimation with Bollas's major theoretical concerns but also to think clinically about sublimation as it pertains to a specifically Freudian clinical practice.

Chapter 4 attempts to read the commentaries of Heidegger, Lacan and the philosopher Bernard Stiegler on Sophocles's *Antigone*, with an ear toward their resonance with one another, and despite their at times considerable differences. None of these thinkers provide a purely literary analysis of the play, and such an analysis is of no concern to me here. Rather, Heidegger, Lacan and Stiegler each see in *Antigone* a way of thinking the question of politics today, and for both Lacan and Stiegler (though in different ways, and more urgently for Stiegler) this question cannot operate without renewing what is meant by sublimation within a psychoanalytic register. Heidegger, Lacan and Stiegler each think *Antigone* in relation to the question of the passage from minority to responsibility that is *adolescence*—a time when those most formative years of infancy and childhood give rise to the first invigorating attempts at *autopoiesis* or self-formation. Read together, these authors offer a way of thinking the power of the revolutionary adolescent spirit as well as the consequences of the destruction of that spirit. Psychoanalysis, I argue, can be conceived as an effort at preparing to reverse this latter trajectory within both contemporary developmental and political contexts.

Finally, Chapter 5 takes up this preparatory ground elaborated in the previous chapter in order to expand a thinking about the consequences of the destruction of the superego and the undermining of the cultivation of capacities for sublimation as dictated by financialization and the rise of what has been called the attention economy, which as a result destroy all attention and all (or, at least, most) finances. The central figure here for understanding the world in which we currently live, and the forms of suffering it imposes on individuals who do or do not seek out clinical intervention, will be Nietzsche. It was Nietzsche who thought the importance of sublimation before Freud, and who was the first to give it its contemporary determination in terms of its relation to the body and to sexuality. Sexuality remains a vastly more complex and crucial subject of contemporary politics than those who reduce it to an object of struggle in the wars over cultural recognition appear capable of grasping—a point I will elaborate in relation to Nietzsche's diagnosis of *nihilism* as the essence of the increasingly unmanageable self-destructive tendencies of our era. Stiegler, whose influence is pervasive throughout the book, and who took up Nietzsche's project and even more insistently drew attention to sublimation as a theory of the intersection of the individual, sexuality and politics, will also be discussed in further depth. This intersection is where psychoanalysis must situate itself today, both as a critical response to the environment in which we now find ourselves (yet without providing just another theoretical basis for the critique of ideology) and as a treatment of choice for those who suffer the misery of being dispirited by a world that expects them to foot the bill for nothing but the paradox of freely purchasable choices, with no alternatives.

★★★

This is my third book. My first book began with the sentence, "What follows is decidedly a hybrid" (Russell 2017, p. xiii). At the time I thought I was referring only to that work, which was an attempt at thinking philosophically about dilemmas I was encountering in my everyday practice as an analyst. I did not anticipate then that such hybridity would define everything I would continue to write (the present volume included), or that it would gradually open up to broader concerns, taking me beyond questions of clinical work, which nonetheless remain the most central questions for me. Hybrid thinking—which cannot escape the mandate of hard work in exposing oneself to the unfamiliar—is what is more and more required today in order to upset boundaries and to redraw lines of opportunity for intelligent, sensitive and rigorously thoughtful dialogue.

Successful hybridity requires creativity on the part of the author, and a tolerance for creativity on the part of the addressee. We do not live in a time that will be remembered for such tolerance, and the status of psychoanalysis today, both internally as a discipline and in relation to the world at large, is sadly reflective of that regrettable fact. Herein lies the meaning of my subtitle: between two deaths. Some readers will recognize this as a formulation of Lacan's (those who don't will be informed of this in Chapter 4, where it will be discussed). But I appropriate this formula more broadly and with regard to the suffocating atmosphere in which psychoanalytic clinicians currently find themselves: between the potential death of an interpretive clinic, and the death of the mind capable of being treated by that clinic—the mind still capable of sublimation.

Extreme creativity is the only viable form of resistance to conditions of extreme control. As it is for Bollas (1999), psychoanalysis to me is just such a form of extreme creativity, even if it doesn't appear so, to the extent that we have been duped into imagining that the practice of creativity is subordinate to the act of cultural production. Attempting to provide a revised understanding of sublimation and of the superego at some point along the way appeared to me as a way of writing about and affirming such extremes.

I will also admit that I lied when I wrote "decidedly." At no point did I ever make any such decision. Or rather, a decision to proceed in this manner was made *for* me, *by* me, according to a structure of self-relation that will be central to my topic here.

8 *Introduction*

Note

1 In the contemporary analytic literature, "concreteness" refers to a state of mind dominated by literalness and the reduction of complexity, precluding the capacity for symbolization and serving as a more primitive means of managing psychic pain in response to the need for immediate gratification (Frosch 2012, p. xix). In contrast, "'symbolization' (or abstraction) refers to a process whereby we can meaningfully understand that an event can be looked at from a variety of perspectives. Symbolization makes it possible to look at a thing in an 'as if' way rather than as 'true' or absolute" (p. xx). It seems to me that what repression was to psychoanalysis in the first half of the twentieth century, and what narcissism was to psychoanalysis as it developed from the 1960s to the mid-1990s, the problem of concreteness or *desymbolization* is becoming to the field today at the beginning of the twenty-first century.

References

Bollas, C. (1999). "Psychoanalysis and Creativity." In: *The Mystery of Things*. New York: Routledge, pp. 167–180.

Freud, S. (1923). *The Ego and the Id*. S.E. XIX, pp. 1–66.

Freud, S. (1927). *The Future of an Illusion*. S.E. XXI, pp. 1–56.

Frosch, A. (Ed.). (2012). *Absolute Truth and Unbearable Psychic Pain*. London: Routledge.

Heidegger, M. (1996). *Being and Time*. Trans. J. Stambaugh. New York: SUNY Press.

Kirk, G.S., Raven, J.E. and Schofield, M. (Eds.). (1983). *The Presocratic Philosophers*, Second Edition. London: Cambridge University Press.

Loewald, H. (1988). *Sublimation: Inquiries into Theoretical Psychoanalysis*. New Haven, CT: Yale University Press.

Russell, J. (2017). *Nietzsche and the Clinic: Psychoanalysis, Philosophy, Metaphysics*. London: Routledge.

1 Freud—sublimation and superego

The aim of this chapter is to provide a close, somewhat speculative (re-constructive) reading of a series of Freud's texts that traces a particular trajectory of the concept of sublimation in Freud's work, one that ultimately culminates in the appearance of the concept of the superego with the advent of the structural model in 1923. My effort is not to rehearse every instance of the appearance of the term over the course of Freud's career, nor is it to tend exclusively to the contradictions inherent to Freud's use of the concept, which so many previous authors have already pointed out (for an overview, see Gemes 2009). Nor is my effort to attempt to resolve these contradictions. Rather, I will attempt to demonstrate that if we pay close attention to the way in which Freud meditates on this concept over the course of a series of coordinated texts at crucial moments in his career, we can appreciate how central the concept of sublimation would become in the development of certain more advanced aspects of his thinking. This will require revaluation of certain other basic Freudian concepts.

The reading I will propose will likely be unwelcome by contemporary orthodox psychoanalytic traditions, both Freudian and anti-Freudian. To be clear, I am not proposing the "correct" way of reading Freud, but a particular way of reading him, through the evolution of a series of particular concepts. That is, I am proposing a creative way of reading Freud on the topic of sublimation, which is to say, a way of sublimating the concept of sublimation in the context of a theoretical scene that has all but dismissed the topic entirely. Reinventing the concept of sublimation—and with it, the concept of the superego, with which it is irreducibly intertwined—today requires a creative, affirmative approach to the inheritance of conceptual and practical traditions. As I will argue, this gesture seems precisely what Freud's conclusions regarding the topic of sublimation prescribe.

The drive and the instinct

Kaplan (1992) offers a thoughtful, comprehensive consideration of the difficulties attending to the concept of sublimation in the history of psychoanalysis, but in the course of his contribution, never does he answer the question posed

DOI: 10.4324/9781003243878-1

10   *Freud—sublimation and superego*

by the essay's title: "What is sublimated in sublimation?" The answer to this question is, in fact, remarkably simple: the drive.

In Freud's work, there is never any question that what is sublimated in sublimation is the drive. The reason this has been such a difficult thought for analysts since Freud is that, beginning in 1923 with the introduction of the structural model, and specifically with the introduction of the concept of the id, the concept of the drive has been confused with the concept of the biological instinct.[1] An adequate post-Freudian theory of sublimation has suffered from this confusion because an instinct is precisely something that cannot be sublimated, whereas a drive is to be distinguished from a biological instinct based on the fact that it is essentially marked by its capacity for sublimation as one of its possible vicissitudes.

As Laplanche (1976) argues, an appreciation of the differences between the Freudian drive and the biological instinct is essential to grasping all of Freud's major insights in the *Three Essays on the Theory of Sexuality,* and why he was to insist on the centrality of the subject's sexual determination up through the posthumously published *An Outline of Psycho-Analysis.* The first Essay is organized around Freud's effort to explain the nature of homosexuality ("inversion") and by extension all "perversions," by demonstrating that the ubiquitousness of perverse behavior is what allows us to derive a concept of a drive as an impulse that has no intrinsic or fixed object. This absence of any fixed object which defines the concept of the drive is in contradistinction to the biological notion of an instinct: Genetically programmed, an instinct never deviates from either its object or its aim. Hunger, for example, can never be satisfied by anything but food, and it cannot be diverted from the satisfaction of nourishment. A drive, however, is defined by Freud precisely in terms of its lacking a pre-programmed object, and by the fact that its aim and its object can change over time.

Homosexuality, for Freud, is therefore neither a biological condition nor a conscious choice. The general field of sexuality, broadly conceived, which is to say beyond the privilege accorded to reproduction demonstrates that a framework which thinks only in terms of these opposed possibilities is thoroughly inadequate: "The nature of inversion is explained neither by the hypothesis that it is innate nor by the alternative hypothesis that it is acquired" (Freud 1905, p. 140). That is, in terms of the field of critical investigation that Freud is attempting to delimit, sexuality is neither a question of conscious choice nor are we "born this way," as virtually all contemporary discourse on sexuality, having become thoroughly politicized after Freud, would have us choose. It is on the basis of the inadequacy of this opposition that Freud will open up an investigation into the dimension of the drive as something that implicates both mind and body. The Freudian concept of the unconscious issues from this insight into a dimension of experience that has neither to do with conscious choice nor with biological determinism. To posit an unconscious is to say that we are driven.

In a well-known passage added in 1915 to the section on the "component

Freud—sublimation and superego   11

instincts [*Triebe*]"—which, Freud says, are "not of a primary nature" (p. 168), which is to say, are not biological, and therefore not instincts but something else—Freud writes,

> By 'instinct' [*Trieb*] is provisionally to be understood the psychical representative of an endosomatic, continuously flowing source of stimulation, as contrasted with a 'stimulus,' which is set up by *single* excitations coming from *without*. The concept of instinct [*Trieb*] is thus one of those lying on the frontier between the mental and the physical. The simplest and likeliest assumption as to the nature of instincts would seem to be that in itself an instinct is without quality, and, so far as mental life is concerned, is only a measure of the demand made upon the mind for work. (p. 168; emphases in original)

The contradictions contained in this passage, which anticipates the turn to biological reductionism inherent to the structural model's concept of the id, issue from Freud's assertion that drives are to be situated on the frontier *between* the mental and the physical, yet at the same time that they are the psychical *representations* of the physical. The appeal to representation, which inherently opposes the psychological and biological domains to one another, undermines the insight that there is a space *between* these two domains to which the concept of the drive provides us access. In one and the same gesture, Freud both indicates a passage beyond and reasserts the primacy of a classical mind/body dualism. The concept of the drive intends to overcome any opposition between body and mind, but in attempting to describe this interstitial divide, Freud appeals to the concept of representation, which reinforces this opposition by thinking in terms of a simple transposition of one domain to another. In North America, this gesture will provide support for the confused and obfuscatory term "instinctual drive" (Brenner 1973).

In saying that a drive is by definition "without quality," which is to indicate its essentially objectless nature, which is in no way the same as denying the essential domain of what are called object relations, Freud is attempting to establish the reality of a "frontier" that is a *between* of mind and body—a domain that both links and separates these classically opposed domains. What defines a drive, and again in contradistinction to biological instincts, is its capacity for diversion or deviation with respect to any object. Instincts are genetically programmed to seek after specific objects. Drives have no such orientation and are subject to aleatory diversions and deviations. To emphasize object relatedness and to say that we are inherently driven to seek after objects is not to revise Freudian theory, but to misrecognize the purpose of the concept of the drive.

The drive as a "demand made upon the mind for work" is typically rendered as an account of what sets the "psychic apparatus" in motion. But we should not be so quick to reduce what Freud means by "work" here to some form of automatic functioning. "Work" here can also be read as a

12 Freud—sublimation and superego

demand for critical judgment, as an openness to an experience of the world. As a demand made upon the mind for work, the concept of the drive attempts to demarcate a frontier that is at once a kind of openness. That is, to be driven is precisely not to be biologically pre-programmed, but to be able to encounter the world as an opportunity for difference, novelty and change. The variability of the drive reflects an originary openness of mind and world, such that to be driven is to be capable of working both on the world and on oneself, and in such a way that to work on the world *is* to work on oneself, and equally the reverse. As I am driven to write at this moment, for instance, I am attempting to contribute something to the world, and in such a way that I transform myself in the process. Writing is not a transposition of something that preexists inside me onto a scene that can be objectively accessed by others. In writing, I am working at the frontier that both separates and connects mind and world, and in a way that disproves all efforts to figure their relation in terms of some absolute opposition. Setting the mind to work means setting the mind to work on a world that it internalizes and that it externalizes itself upon in turn.

This was already presupposed in the very concept of sublimation, which had preceded and conditioned the emergence of the psychoanalytic project, most essentially in the work of Goethe, and then in the work of Nietzsche, who gave the concept its contemporary determination as having to do with the body and with sexuality (Kaufman 2013, pp. 218–223). In a certain sense, the very concept of the drive as something other than a biological instinct is a response to the question as to what is sublimated in sublimation. With the concept of the drive, Freud had attempted to provide a scientific basis for answering this question. Without the concept of sublimation as it was already circulating prior to Freud's efforts, Freud might not have even been led to posit the concept of the drive as a means of resisting all classical oppositions of mind and body. The concept of sublimation precedes and determines all of Freud's contributions where the investigation and the expansion of our understanding of sexuality is concerned.

The drive and the dream

As Laplanche (1976) further demonstrates, Freud's argument in the *Three Essays* concerns the way in which the drive is derived from the genetically programmed biological instinct in having originally been "propped up" on instinctual experience in a relation of "leaning" (*Anlehnung*). Operating mechanically according to feeding mechanisms, the infant eventually discovers not only the pleasures involved in stimulating its mouth while suckling at the breast but also its capacity to provide itself with those pleasures even in the absence of the breast. The erotic stimulation intrinsic to the mechanical feed becomes the basis upon which the infant discovers a capacity to give itself a pleasure that is supplementary to, and in excess of, the experience of feeding. Putting its thumb in its mouth, the hungry baby discovers a capacity to

Freud—sublimation and superego   13

provide for itself oral stimulation, and in this way, it discovers a nascent sense of itself as an active agency for the very first time.

The repetitive nature of the feed is the condition of possibility of the discovery of the self as what can *give itself* the pleasure that the feed supplementarily provides. This primitive emergence of the agency of the self is an act of discovery according to which the self in this way gives itself to itself from out of the repetition of need (hunger) to which it is irreducibly subjected. At these moments, the drive begins to drift from instinctually programmed patterns and to constitute new opportunities for what will eventually emerge as capacities for self-care. The emergence of auto-erotism from out of a primitive, biologically pre-determined integration of mind and environment describes the constitution of the drive as something other than a mere instinct. In portraying the derivation of the drive from the instinct in this way, Freud prefigures what Mahler et al. (1975) would later describe as the psychological birth of the human infant.

Freud's effort in demonstrating the emergence of the drive from the biological instinct is thus not to derive the mind from the body, but to open a field of investigation in which the relations of mind and body can be scientifically sketched out in a way that does not from the outset proceed from a classical framework that assumes mind and body stand formally opposed. This is how Freud distinguishes his approach to mind as a concept distinct from the concept of the soul in order to retain a properly scientific orientation. In positing the concept of the drive, Freud's project is to undermine any such opposition in its having becoming naturalized even within a scientific framework that professes to reject the concept of the soul and of any approach to the mind based on such a concept. In continuing to oppose mind and body, while regretting that contemporary science has yet to have "solved" this problem as to their intrinsic connection, the contemporary sciences of mind fail to appreciate Freud's appeal to a science of sexuality as a "solution" to the intransigent problems of classical mind/body dualism.

A thinking about the drive as belonging to a *third area* was always an attempt to think a relation of mind and body, as well as a relation of mind-body and world, in terms other than that of an opposition. The Freudian articulation of the essentially objectless nature of the drive, or rather, its aleatory constitution with regard to object relations, which are otherwise obvious and undeniable, was an attempt to define a domain of experience in which the biological instincts' inherent relatedness to objects capable of providing satisfaction for uncircumventible need was intrinsically surmounted and overcome by biological necessity itself. Drives are by definition in excess of biological need; this is why they are essentially and originally chaotic in nature.

This is also what, as Freud will state categorically in the short but extremely sophisticated 1911 paper on "The Two Principles of the Mental Functioning," determines the drive as the catalyst in the constitution of the dimension of fantasy. It is the capacity for fantasy that will distinguish the human from the animal, as an excessive articulation of the human being's capacity for memory,

14 *Freud—sublimation and superego*

which the animal does not possess to any comparably sophisticated degree. For Freud, what defines human being is not sexuality but memory, of which sexuality is a particular and decisive articulation. This is expressed in the Freudian concept of the drive as again distinct from the biological instinct: Without a predetermined or programmed object, the drive animates the domain of fantasy as a form of memory that projects a future of possibility that might be realized (or not). Fantasy is originally a way of experiencing the past as if it were the present—a form of memory. This is what the infant is doing when it hallucinates the presence of the breast while giving itself the pleasure of thumbsucking. Gradually—which is to say, according to a *process* of development, which is never simply given internally but environmentally determined—this constitutes the capacity to project a future in which fantasies can be realized as realities, through which desires can come to fruition. This is the "work" that the drive initially and essentially sets upon the mind. And this is the basis of the possibility of what will become sublimation. The concept of sublimation is implicitly central to Freud's thinking about the concept of the drive in the *Three Essays on the Theory of Sexuality*. Sexuality will remain a lifelong preoccupation for Freud precisely because it demonstrates that domain in which oppositions between mind and body are no longer tenable.

Having established the central role of fantasy in human life—a role that distinguishes, again for Freud, the human from the animal, for which memory does not play such an essential and constitutive role—Freud will spend years not ignoring the centrality of object relations in human life, but insistently arguing for the importance of fantasy, which is rooted in the hallucinatory capacity of the hungry baby, based on its capacity for memorization, and which will constitute its capacity to project a future, which will become a future *for itself*. Fantasy, which begins as a form of memory retrieval, at once founds the capacity to think ahead, which is to say to *desire* something in excess of what the child is in possession of or is bringing into being in the present moment. This had been what dreams or the function of dreaming had revealed to Freud.

When Freud announced in 1900 that the dream is the fulfillment of a wish—a discovery that he tells Fliess causes him to dream that one day the location of this discovery will be inscribed with his name and the date of his breakthrough—this was to say that dreaming is in fact a form of *thinking*. Sensory in nature, the dream dissimulates itself as a form of thinking on the part of the subject because we traditionally associate thinking with consciousness and with the phenomenon of the inner voice, that is, with language. The dream, Freud recognizes, is itself a different kind of thinking, one that articulates itself hallucinatorily because it is otherwise and constitutively inaccessible to consciousness. It is not that there is some hidden language of dreams—this is the promise on which *The Interpretation of Dreams* is marketed, but one on which it demonstrates from the outset that it will refuse to deliver, that of providing some universal key according to which dreams can be deciphered—but that we must expand our notion of thinking in order

Freud—sublimation and superego 15

to encompass what Freud will later, in 1911, call *originally unconscious thought* (p. 221). Dreams reveal that thinking cannot be equated with consciousness, that there is a form of thinking that transpires outside the subject's conscious self-awareness. Freud will never stop insisting on the radical nature of this discovery, and he will blame rejections of psychoanalysis in principle—especially by philosophers—on a refusal to accept this possibility.

Libidinal economy

If dreaming is a form of thinking, and if such thinking constitutes a form of wish-fulfillment, this means that, for Freud, thinking is originally and essentially a form of desire.[2] Breaking with the classical tradition which, since the foundation of Western thought as practiced by the ancient Greeks has identified the essence of thought as reason, Freud's argument is that prior to the articulations of reason, and even prior to the introduction of language into the psychic economy of the *in-fans*, thinking originally consists in the capacity to formulate wishes: to formulate, however rudimentarily, the presence of something that is absent yet desirable (for instance, the breast). Negating the absence of the desirable non-present object, unconscious thought is at the same time that through which will be constituted the capacity to imagine any horizon of future possibility. When the breast is absent, the infant finds itself capable of retrieving the perceptual presence of the object of desire by "hypercathecting" or libidinally investing in its memories of previous instances of satisfaction to the point of hallucinatory intensity. It is this capacity to which we regress every night in the formation of the dream hallucination. The dream hallucination is a form of wishing, which is a form of memory, which we no longer recognize as such but which dream phenomena indicate we never at any point abandon.

The unconscious, in the mode of what will later be termed the id, as the seat of the drives, will in this way begin to organize itself, which is to say to formulate an *economy* of the drives. What will become psychic structure is originally this economizing tendency, as a process of self-organization. Economizing the drives as the mode of originally unconscious thought means that the infant moves from simply wishing, to wishing *for something*. As Freud will elaborate in "The Two Principles of Mental Functioning," from this effort at psychic self-organization—provoked by the demands of reality but inaugurated by the drives themselves, as what will "put the mind to work"—will proceed the cultivation of cognition as the coordination of memory, attention, judgment, reality testing, and so forth. This is the process of the formation of the self or ego, and it is why a rigorously Freudian thinking can never legitimately be reconciled with those who will posit the existence of a rudimentary ego structure present at birth. This latter position contradicts everything Freud argues for from *The Interpretation of Dreams* to the *Three Essays on the Theory of Sexuality*, to the papers on

16 *Freud—sublimation and superego*

metapsychology, passing through *The Ego and the Id* and up until the posthumously published *An Outline of Psycho-Analysis*. The idea of a nascent ego structure present at birth returns us to a classical, pre-Freudian position that once again opposes mind and body, relinquishing the breakthrough of the topographical model, and giving rise to what Loewald will call, as I will discuss at length in Chapter 2, a "creationist view of the world" (1988, p. 5).

This self-organizing or auto-economizing of the drives, in this way become desire in its most elementary form, is what will relate the infant to the world in the creative constitution of the world—initially, the world of the dream— which is thus simultaneously the process of the constitution of the self. It is again simply untrue that Freud ever failed to recognize that we are instinctively, biologically oriented to seek out relations with other human beings (what Darwinian doesn't know that?); but from 1900 to 1911, Freud will not concern himself with this obvious trait shared by all living organisms with regard to their species. Instead, he will focus his research on how the function of dreaming, having become the capacity to fantasize—which escapes the influence of the reality principle in being "split off," becoming the proper province of the unconscious, but also of daydreams—will constitute a way of withdrawing from engagement with the world in a way that he will see forms the pathogenic basis of neurosis.

Beginning in 1911, however, with the "Two Principles" paper—indeed, beginning with its very first paragraph, which ends, "And now we are confronted with the task of investigating the development of the relation of neurotics and of mankind in general to reality, and of bringing the psychological significance of the real external world into the structure of our theories"—Freud will become preoccupied with how dreaming, having become fantasizing, *also* forms the very basis on which we relate to the world. It is this question—of how the capacity to dream, in which we find a basis for understanding pathological world-withdrawal, is *at the same time* the basis on which we become capable of relating to reality (the question of which, in *Civilization and Its Discontents*, will become that of the world in a more refined sense)—that will implicitly inform all of Freud's major theoretical statements for the rest of his career, especially the working out of the structural model in 1923. That is, beginning in 1911, Freud begins to think the paradox of how fantasy, as what *disrupts* our relation to the world, is at the same time what *constitutes* our relation to the world in a specifically human way.

To say that dreams are the fulfillment of a wish was to say that dreaming is a form of thinking, and that thinking is a form of wishing—of cultivating a sense of the future. Thinking depends upon a sense of the future in which dreams can be realized. The capacity to think, which is to say to think *for oneself*, is rooted in the capacity to fantasize, which is a capacity to dream not just of a *past* but of a *future* that is happening as if it were *now*, until this fantasized future and the present moment coincide, from out of the sense of oneself as an individual. This is what the concept of sublimation, before Freud, and before the determination of the specificity of the concept of the drive as the essence of a specifically human sexuality, as a form of memory, which makes it possible for human beings to *fall* in love with one another in an element of repetition (e.g., "the finding of an object is always a refinding of it" (Freud 1905, p. 145)), had already established.

When drives oriented toward immediate gratification are economized, they become desire, which is the basis for our capacity not only to relate to but also to *participate* in the world in such a way that we are able to *contribute* to it. Desire always and fundamentally involves being captivated by some aspect of the world beyond ourselves, and in such a way that both depends upon and cultivates our sense that there is a future horizon which we not only imagine we can achieve but also that we learn actively to take pleasure in working toward, even though doing so is fundamentally in contradiction to what Freud had called the pleasure principle. In 1920, Freud would call this Eros, in contrast to a death drive which is a generalized regressive orientation of all drives toward disorganization and toward imitating the biological automaticity of what are otherwise called instincts.

The future of narcissism

A thorough survey of Freud's papers on metapsychology is beyond the scope of this short study. It is still worth rehearsing the place that the concept of sublimation occupied for Freud during the general period of this famously concentrated effort at summarizing psychoanalytic findings for the scientific community, with which Freud strongly identified and to which he aspired to become a recognized and exalted member. In his Editor's Introduction to the series of five papers published in the Standard Edition under the heading "Papers on Metapsychology," James Strachey reconstructs the weeks of intensive creativity that led to the publication of these papers between 1915 and 1917. These essays form the centerpiece of Freud's theoretical writings and were an attempt by Freud "to provide a stable theoretical foundation for psychoanalysis" (S.E. XIV, p. 101). Strachey reports that Freud had intended to collect these papers together with several others in a volume to be titled *Zur Vorbereitung einer Metapsychologie* (*Preliminaries to a Metapsychology*) for the purpose of providing such a foundation, and likely as a way of securing his discoveries from the divergences of former colleagues like Jung and Adler.

The demarcation of these papers from other texts in which Freud offers purely theoretical reflections is suspect but has passed into the general reception of Freud's work. Strachey groups the papers together based solely on the historical period during which they were written. We learn from Ernest Jones that the papers were all written in a brief period of seven weeks between 15 March and 4 May 1915 (p. 102). This period of remarkable productivity has become a part of the Freud legend, and perhaps rightfully so, but referring to these papers as the papers on metapsychology—as if there were no others—too neatly divorces them from those preceding papers on the topic of metapsychological research. It also tends to conceal the fact that, as Strachey

18   *Freud—sublimation and superego*

indicates, again citing Jones, "seven more papers were added to the series during the following three months, the whole collection of twelve being completed by 9 August" (p. 102)—unpublished papers that do not survive and that were likely later destroyed by their author. In 1915, Freud appears to have been doing quite a bit of sublimating. In relation to a comment he made in a letter to J.J. Putnam—"I myself am using the break in my work [due to the war] at this time to finish off a book containing a collection of twelve psychological essays" (p. 102, fn 1; editor's brackets)—one wonders whether this period of furious productivity did not in fact have everything to do with his ability to sublimate his response to contemporary political events.

Strachey links the five official papers on metapsychology first to the famously difficult Seventh Chapter of *The Interpretation of Dreams* (1900), and then retroactively to the "Project" of 1895 which also remained unpublished during Freud's lifetime but which was not destroyed—a curious fact given the fate of the seven unseen papers on metapsychology. Others texts included in this series are the paper on "The Two Principles of Mental Functioning," part three of the Schreber case study, as well as the papers on "The Unconscious" and "On Narcissism: An Introduction."

Of the seven missing papers prepared during the summer of 1915, Strachey demonstrates that by the time of publication of the last of the papers on metapsychology in 1917, Freud appeared still to have intended to publish the remaining seven, but that by 1919 there is evidence in his correspondence with Lou Andreas-Salomé that he had judged them to be unsatisfactory. Of the topics with which they were to have dealt, Strachey demonstrates with confidence that they covered consciousness, anxiety, conversion hysteria, obsessional neurosis, and the transference neuroses. He then states with the same confidence that, "We can even guess the subjects which the two unspecified papers may have discussed—namely, Sublimation and Projection (or Paranoia)" (S.E. XIV, p. 103).

Here then is the specific location of the "lacuna" cited by Laplanche and Pontalis (1973, p. 433) in Freud's thought with regard to a worked-out theory of sublimation. I cannot pretend to speculate as to why Freud might have judged these works unsatisfactory, nor if, had the paper on sublimation appeared, it would have made its development (or lack thereof) in the secondary literature any more coherent. Perhaps it was this paper in particular that presented Freud with such difficulty and that caused him to judge negatively the remaining six worked out at this time. Judging by the relevance of the concept to virtually all of the other papers on metapsychology, it seems safe to assume that the other six missing papers would have employed this concept as well, making the paper on sublimation particularly central for the projected twelve-essay volume.

"On Narcissism" (1914) does not officially belong to this creative period in Freud's career, but it deserves to be read alongside the surviving papers on metapsychology, as does the "Two Principles" paper of 1911, both of which contain references to sublimation. In it, we find Freud taking stock of where psychoanalysis was at and where it should be headed during a tumultuous time both for Europe and for the world generally. In 1914, Freud is at the center of what is becoming an international movement. Previous followers are now developing in their own directions. Freud's main concern will be to defend the importance of the libido theory for a properly psychoanalytic science. This will require some modifications to take account of new observations that the success of psychoanalysis so far had made possible.

The opening gesture of the essay's argument is typical of Freud. Appropriating the term from Paul Näcke, who had used it to describe a form of perversion, Freud demonstrates that a narcissistic position is actually common to the development of the libido so that what appears to be a marginal phenomenon is actually ubiquitous: "Narcissism in this sense would not be a perversion, but the libidinal complement to the egoism of the instinct of self-preservation, a measure of which may justifiably be attributed to every living creature" (1914, pp. 73–74). Self-preservation, which he had previously ascribed to an ego drive, in contradiction to a sexual drive itself the repository of libido, will be rethought as an intrinsically libidinal effort—as self-love or as self-care. Such libidinized self-care can be ascribed "to every living creature."

Rehearsing the distinction between the sexual instincts (*Triebe*) and the instincts of the ego or of self-preservation, Freud asserts that neurosis arises when the sexual instincts predominate over the ego instincts because a fantasy has been substituted for a reality. Freud will show that this is a kind of narcissistic gesture: Neuroses are at bottom narcissistic conditions, as are psychoses. This is Freud's preliminary effort to establish a way of thinking comprehensively about the relationship between neurosis and psychosis.[3] In positing a primary form of narcissism anterior to any secondary pathological manifestation, Freud writes,

> Thus we form the idea of there being an original libidinal cathexis of the ego, from which some is later given off to objects, but which fundamentally persists and is related to the object-cathexes much as the body of an amoeba is related to the pseudopodia which it puts out. (p. 75)

This is to indicate that originally, investment in the self and investment in the object are the *same* gesture: self-care is other-care, and vice versa. In the reciprocal circuit of the mother-infant relationship, and for both parties, loving the other is the same as loving the self. Such circuits of libidinal economy are circuits of differentiated integration in which the partners cannot be thought of as formally opposed to one another (as Winnicott gave us to think when he famously stated, "There is no such thing as an infant" (1960, p. 587)).[4] Again, love for the other and love for the self are in essence the same gesture in the context of the circuit or system of primary narcissism.

And yet, in the very same paragraph, Freud will posit an *antithesis* between what he will for the first time describe as ego-libido and object-libido. In attempting to modify the framework that had opposed the ego instincts and

20 Freud—sublimation and superego

the sexual instincts, Freud nonetheless continues to defer to a vocabulary of antithesis and opposition, even while indicating that this way of thinking is only provisional. This is yet another typical (though this time highly unfortunate) Freudian gesture: What appear to be opposed are actually foundationally integrated. This was also the case in 1911 with regard to what Freud had to say about the relationship between the pleasure principle and the reality principle (Freud 1911, p. 219, fn 1).

This form of argument will persist when Freud goes on, in the second section of the narcissism paper, to distinguish between "anaclitic" and "narcissistic" types of object choice, which he will call masculine and feminine types, though he will not divide these exclusively between biological men and women. Anaclitic object choice involves loving and being devoted to the object, while narcissistic object choice has to do with the wish to be loved as a way of loving oneself. In no way are these gestures to be conceived of as opposed. The entire point of the essay is to demonstrate that, in no longer being capable of submitting to some opposition between ego instincts and sexual instincts—indicating that each implies and cannot be conceived of as existing in the absence of the other—the narcissistic/object libido distinction is an effort to overcome a classical, dialectical logic.

It is in the context of this distinction that Freud makes a remark worth attending to with regard to the concept of sublimation, which will be central to the third and final section of the essay. In providing a schematic overview of the various types of object choice, Freud writes that among the narcissistic types according to which a person may love is the choice to love "what he himself would like to be" (1914, p. 90). It is this comment that will set up all of Freud's reflections in Section III of "On Narcissism," where he will introduce the notion of the ego ideal which, passing by way of "Mourning and Melancholia" and *Group Psychology and the Analysis of the Ego*, will culminate in the introduction of the concept of the superego in Chapter 3 of *The Ego and the Id*.

Freud's idea here implicates time, and most specifically a sense of the future. Choosing (unconsciously) to love "what he himself would like to be" depends on the child's emergent sense of a horizon of future possibility over the course of which he will not only passively develop but actively *individuate* himself. Freud is indicating that the child's sense that there is not only a future, but a future of the self, which is at once to say of the world, over which the child can exert some degree of control emerges from out of this primary narcissistic matrix—which is a matrix of *relations*, though not of relations between subjects and objects in an ordinary sense—in which investment in the self and investment in the other are one and the same. This is an economy in which the libido flows not from the self to the object, but between two figures differentiated and integrated both mutually and each within themselves, forming a complex circuit of relationality that cannot be thought according to a classical logic of opposition or antithesis. It is this logic that insistently confounds efforts on the part of psychoanalysis, again beginning with Freud himself, to elaborate a coherent theory of sublimation.

Freud—sublimation and superego 21

It is in the final section of the narcissism paper that Freud introduces the concept of the ego ideal, which is inescapably bound to a discussion of the concept of sublimation, according to which a self engaged in an act of idealization, "*projects before him* as his ideal … the substitute for the lost narcissism of his childhood in which he was his own ideal" (p. 94; emphasis added). All capacities for sublimation are dependent upon the self's capacity to project before itself a horizon of future possibility in which desire can be realized. Today we must think this as the essence of sublimation because it is this capacity that is being ruined by the ways in which civilization and culture are currently organized.

The constitution of an ideal is the constitution of a future self—which, again, always implies a future world—that we project before us, toward a future that does not yet exist, but that thenceforth does exist *in fantasy*, which is to say in our dreams, and in relation to which we can begin the long process of disciplining ourselves so as to individuate ourselves accordingly. As the child grows and becomes an adult, and in coming to terms with both its proclivities and its limitations, it projects forward an ideal state that preserves the fantasies of the past by investing in a future toward which it strives, and in terms of which its activities are organized. If the child in the process of becoming an adult remains committed to these activities, the fantasies of the past will have remained active as dreams that are realized in the dimension of the future, which does not exist until it is made to do so, by means of the faculty of dreaming and of capacities for self-discipline. Without these capacities to project a worthwhile future in which we are capable of realizing our desires—that is, *to make our dreams come true*—the world can only appear as the source of an immense misery and despair or, as I will demonstrate in my last chapter, an object of absolute hatred to be ruthlessly destroyed.

The projection of future possibility is what Freud's concept of idealization here consists in (this is to be distinguished from other uses of the term by Freud, such as in the *Three Essays* where he discusses perversion as the "idealization of the instinct" (Freud 1905, p. 161)), and it is an essential part of that process of sublimation whereby the drives become desire. Idealization is not just the projection of a future, but the projection of a future that is conceived of as intrinsically *good,* which is to say a source of reward which is not that of immediate gratification. Idealization projects drive-based enjoyment beyond the immediacy of the *now*.

Sublimation concerns the drive; idealization concerns the object, especially where the object is at bottom indistinguishable from the self (and therefore is not an "object" strictly speaking). This latter point is what Freud will clarify with the introduction of the concept of *identification* in "Mourning and Melancholia." In idealization and sublimation, we are always measuring ourselves against our fantasized pasts and our projected futures. This is the fundamental way in which human beings, in having become civilized, regulate their affects and their behavior. It is not only possible but common to be possessed of the one capacity in the absence of the other: The person who is

22 Freud—sublimation and superego

capable of forming ideals, but who is incapable of living up to them by sub-limating toward the realization of their desire is the clinically ubiquitous patient who enters analysis complaining that their lives did not go the way they imagined they would. The person capable of sublimation, but who has no strong sense of taking pleasure in the realization of ideals, is the one who is often referred to as "wasted talent" (Rimbaud comes to mind).

Before moving on to other texts of Freud, allow me to make two suggestions, both concerning the problems that analysts have always encountered in the effort to think sublimation coherently. The first concerns the problem, over which a great deal of ink has been spilled, as to whether or not sublimation constitutes a "desexualization" of the libido. "Desexualization of the libido" would seem a perplexing contradiction in terms, but if sublimation does not involve something of the sort, then sublimated activities cannot be thought otherwise than as ordinary neurotic symptoms, to be distinguished only by the fact that their outcomes are socially and culturally valued. Freud's concept of idealization, however, in the sense to which he gives it in "Mourning and Melancholia" and later in *The Ego and the Id*, offers a way of obviating this question by stating that rather than becoming "desexualized," the self and its capacity for achievement is idealized, and that this forms a core element of the capacity to sublimate the drive such that it becomes desire, thereby linking self and world—*through* fantasy, although fantasy is precisely that which *detaches* us from the world.

Second, a related and again confounding problem in the literature concerns whether or not sublimation is itself a form of repression, or if it necessarily depends on a prior act of repression. Here again, Freud himself appears to point the way. He writes,

> The development of the ego consists in a departure from primary narcissism and gives rise to a vigorous attempt to recover that state. This departure is brought about by means of the displacement of libido on to an ego ideal imposed from without, and satisfaction is brought about from fulfilling this ideal. (1914, p. 100)

If this is the case, would it not seem that the motor of ego development is sublimation itself, which is to say that sublimation is not just one psychical activity among others, but the very means by which the self *as* self comes into being, by giving itself structure in relation to the ways in which it interacts with its environment? This is to say that, in a certain sense, sublimation *is* ego formation,[5] which means it should never have made any sense to think that the ego or self could develop somehow outside its fundamental relation to others, beyond the primary caregivers and including the world generally.

Furthermore, when Freud writes, "For the ego the formation of an ideal would be the conditioning factor of repression" (p. 92), does this not indicate that, rather than repression being a precondition for sublimation, sublimation is in fact the precondition of repression? It is this implicit notion

Freud—sublimation and superego 23

that will link Chapter 3 of *The Ego and the Id* to everything Freud will have to say in *Civilization and Its Discontents*, where the central question is what happens when we are deprived of the capacity to sublimate our drives into desire, or when there is regression on an immense social scale from desire to the drives, the result being the unleashing of unmanageably destructive forces—a horizon of future possibility that by 1930 Freud could no longer circumvent himself from projecting.

Superego

By 1923, *sublimation, idealization* and *identification*, in the specific senses to which he had given these terms, have coalesced for Freud into an integrated conceptual economy. This coordination will allow him to think the concept of the superego, to which we must now turn our attention via a careful reading of Chapter 3 of *The Ego and the Id*. Such a reading will demonstrate that the superego cannot be reduced to the moral conscience, nor can it be reduced, as for Lacan, to a "pure culture of the death instinct" (Freud 1923, p. 53)—although it can be rendered as such, as Freud had already outlined in "Mourning and Melancholia" in relation to the topic of suicide. That aspect of the Freudian concept of the superego—the ego ideal—which is not often enough reflected upon today, will be crucial for furthering our understanding of sublimation and of why it is a necessary concept today.[6]

The terminological shift that will see Freud privileging the term superego (*Über-Ich*) has not yet taken place, and from the very title of the chapter Freud retains the earlier term ego ideal: "The considerations that led us to assume the existence of a grade in the ego, a differentiation within the ego, which may be called the 'ego ideal' or 'superego,' have been stated elsewhere. They still hold good" (p. 28). It is not exactly the case, however, that Freud uses these terms throughout the chapter as interchangeably as he appears to suggest at the outset. There is a recognizable difference between the ways in which these two terms are deployed by Freud such that, when superego becomes the predominant term, and the ego ideal—and thus the process of idealization—is relegated to background status in the naturalization of the structural model, this aspect of Freud's thinking about the superego gets lost. It is this aspect to which we must attend, and in conjunction with a new thinking about sublimation, which would thus also entail a new thinking about what Freud had intended with the concept of the superego.

Freud begins by introducing once again the topic of identification, with which he had been able to think states of depression, and which was in fact the central topic of his *Group Psychology and the Analysis of the Ego* from 1921. Having recognized the central role that this process plays in the formation of the child's psyche, Freud installs it at the core of his understanding of the libidinal relation to the object: "At the very beginning ... object–cathexis and identification are no doubt indistinguishable from each other" (Freud 1923, p. 29). This is a repetition of the claim concerning primary narcissism, where

24   *Freud—sublimation and superego*

investment in the other is investment in the self, and in such a way that complicates any effort at opposing self and other within the generalized framework of the subjective and the objective. Freud's attempt is to think this situation more rigorously, in order to understand how this can produce alterations or *differentiations* (p. 28) within the psyche, thereby creating what he is now thinking in terms of psychic structure. If object-cathexis and identification are originally indistinguishable, what this means is that, for Freud, and contrary to his mischaracterization as a "one person psychologist" in the contemporary relational literature, what we call object relations are thoroughly fundamental to the formation of a structured mind.

In relating to the other through identification *with* the other, the child *becomes other than herself*, and in this way she *becomes herself* over the course of development and gradually in relation to the world beyond that of the primary caregivers. This always involves a loss on the part of the id with regard to the objects of the drives. Freud will think this loss most explicitly from the perspective of the question of the Oedipal situation, but we must not miss the fact that he is situating identification among the most essential psychical mechanisms from the very outset, one that governs the process of psychic structuralization in advance, and that will lay the foundations for the formation of character prior to anything like the advent of Oedipal object relations. "From another point of view," Freud writes, prefiguring Oedipal dynamics, which is to say object relations in a formally psychological sense,

> it may be said that this transformation of an erotic object-choice into an alteration of the ego is also a method by which the ego can obtain control over the id and deep its relations with it—at the cost, it is true, of acquiescing to a large extent in the id's experiences. When the ego assumes the features of the object, it is forcing itself, so to speak, upon the id as a love-object and is trying to make good the id's loss by saying: 'Look, you can move me too—I am so like the object.' (p. 30)

Modifying itself through the identificatory "taking in" of the object (which precisely cannot be an "object" in the traditional sense where this is the case, and where identification does not rest upon but *creates* the possibility of an experience of something like "taking in"), the ego presents itself to the id (the drives) as the "object" of potential libidinal investment. This constitutes the originary libidinal circuit of self-care that can go on to become self-respect as the psyche becomes more and more structured via further identifications, which are thus also means by which the mind internalizes prohibitions, thereby economizing the drives by introducing order into chaos. To "obtain control" over the drives, as an effort prior to the advent of repression, means first and foremost to structure the mind in such a way that loops the libido into a circuit of self-investment that is the basis for the possibility of psychological health. The transformation of object-libido into narcissistic-libido is again not predicated on an opposition between two different kinds of libido; it is a

Freud—sublimation and superego   25

question rather of two different *organizations* that the *economics* of the libido—which is *precisely what the concept of psychic structure means*—can assume: a logic of economic investment and, following on the alterations in the ego to appeal to the id by means of identification with aspects of an environment that is fundamentally shared, return.

It is at this point in the text that Freud invokes the concept of sublimation, and in a striking way. He writes,

> The transformation of object-libido into narcissistic libido which thus takes place obviously implies a kind of abandonment of sexual aims, a desexualization—a kind of sublimation, therefore. Indeed, the question arises, and deserves careful consideration, whether this is not the universal road to sublimation, whether all sublimation does not take place place through the mediation of the ego, which begins by changing sexual object-libido into narcissistic libido and then, perhaps, goes on to give it another aim. (p. 30)

This statement is striking for two reasons. First, because when Freud equates this transformation with "a kind of sublimation," it is clear that he does not mean that sublimation is not a deployment of the libido. It is not a question, for Freud, of "desexualized libido" in a strict sense, but of the transposition of erotic *aims* toward aims that cannot be regarded as erotic in an ordinary sense (and there is no such ordinary sense, for Freud), as in the case of a primary investment of care in the self. The secondary literature on sublimation has agonized over what it would mean to say that sublimation involves a desexualized pursuit of aims that belong to the valuation of the cultural sphere. Freud is clearly articulating that such pursuits *are* intrinsically libidinally motivated, that what is "desexualized" is the *aim*, not the *object* in its having become something other than an object of recognizable erotic enjoyment. Sublimation concerns a relationship to an other that is prior to any relation of a subject to an object, as is the case with the self's relation to itself. By means of sublimation, the aim of the drive becomes something other than the pleasure of immediate gratification, whereby the child first discovers pleasure in deferring gratification, enduring the tension of immediately unrealized aims in the service of actualizing future possibility. This is what it would mean for sublimation to be conceived as the conversion of the drives into desire.

Second, Freud's hesitant reference to "a kind of sublimation" indicates that in this instance he is thinking sublimation outside the traditional bounds of a thinking about adherence to recognized cultural ideals. Sublimation here has nothing to do with any ordinary concept of belonging to the social as a domain of intersubjectivity, or as a dimension of experience dependent upon any concept of an enclosed, subjective self. He is suggesting that sublimation is an intrinsic and essential part of the process of the formation of psychic structure. When the ego alters or differentiates itself by means of gestures of identification, and in order to appeal to the id for the purpose of creating libidinal circuits of reciprocal self-investment, *this is itself a form of sublimation*, which is thus a manner by means of which the psyche constitutes itself by structuring itself, such that it becomes capable of projecting a future for itself that it is capable of *living up to—realizing itself* by *realizing its dreams.* Identifying with the other means differentiating oneself in order to make dreams become real—that is to say, *true*—and in such a way that recognizes truth as a value that bears meaning, in being something other than a mere fact, by constituting a future of potential or possibility in which *we will see what happens,* and in which this relationship to risk, chance and uncertainty can be tolerated. An instinct cannot tolerate this uncertainty, as it is dominated by the need for gratification which Freud had called the pleasure principle; the variability of the drive is the primitive and unstructured openness to uncertainty, which must be sublimated.

The cultivation of the capacity to tolerate risk, chance and uncertainty occurs by means of the primitive ego's diverting of the libidinal energy of the drives into what is becoming (but which does not preexist as) the self as an object of investment, opening up an experience of self-as-other by repetitively investing in a *process of becoming* (transformative, individuating development) that registers the horizon of a future worth committing to and investing in. What is sublimated in sublimation is thus not just the drive but the self, where these terms can no longer be conceived in opposition to one another, but must be understood as differentiated articulations of the *same* process that either realizes or fails to realize its aims according to a projected future horizon of desire that is called *autonomy,* after the Greek words *autos* and *nomos*: the conjunction of the act of self-giving (*autos*) and law (*nomos*). This would be, in Freudian terms, the conjunction of auto-erotism and the cultivation of psychic structure, by means of an economizing of the libido through acts of primary repetition—acts of self-investment by means of which a self comes to be in the first place—that would be the essence of sublimation, and that would make possible the achievement of mature, critical reason, which is not a genetic given but a developmental potential or possibility. This is also to say that this possibility is fragile and must be safeguarded lest it might not be realized, which it always might not be.

Processes of sublimation and identification are thus inextricably implicated for Freud, and his continued deference to the concept of the ego ideal indicates that processes of *idealization* form an essential part of this dynamic triumvirate that will make it possible for him to introduce the structural model, according to which the mind can be *differentiated*—become different from or other than itself, while remaining itself—which is to say *structured*. The concept of psychic structure is equivalent to a capacity for psychic differentiation, according to which the psyche enables itself to become itself in becoming-other-than itself. This is what the Freudian concept of identification retains, beyond the reduction of the drive to the biological instinct implied by the concept of the id. At the very same moment that it reduces the concept of the drive—as what originally opens us onto the possibility of future

Freud—sublimation and superego   27

projection—to inborn, and therefore biological instinct, Freud's thought in 1923 is more open than it ever has been to thinking the influence of the instinctual orientation toward external objects. But what is at stake here is a non-oppositional thinking concerning the relationship between the drive and its object, which must be thought otherwise than in classical terms.

Soon after bringing the concept of sublimation to bear on the question of psychic structuralization via processes of identification, Freud writes,

> But, whatever the character's later capacity for resisting the influences of abandoned object-cathexes may turn out to be, *the effects of the first identifications made in childhood will be general and lasting*. This leads us back to the origin of the ego ideal; for behind it there lies hidden an individual's first and most important identification, his identification with the father in his own personal prehistory. *This is apparently not in the first instance the consequence or outcome of an object-cathexis; it is a direct and immediate identification and takes place earlier than any object-cathexis*. But the object-choices belonging to the first sexual period and relating to the father and mother seem normally to find their outcome in an identification of this kind, and would thus reinforce the *primary* one. (p. 31; emphases added)

Freud's attachment to the privilege of the figure of the father here in the context of the boy's development is countered by a footnote which supplements this passage and indicates, "Perhaps it would be safer to say 'with the parents'..." (ibid., fn 1) This is because he is discussing the earliest psychological state in which sexual difference is registered but has yet to be symbolized. When he writes toward the end of the paragraph, "But the object-choices belonging to the first sexual period and relating to the father and mother ...," he is discussing identification in an ordinary sense, once the figure of the object as external to the subjective psyche has been established. But what is at stake here is the question of a *primary* identification, which operates in what "On Narcissism" had called the period of *primary* narcissism, in which there are relations of mutual difference and otherness which cannot yet be conceived on the spatial model of an internal subject opposed to an external object. Primary identifications are prior to object-cathexes because they concern a nascent experience of self that is not yet opposed to the figure of the object, and in such a way that, again, the relation to the other is intrinsically a *transformation* of what is becoming a self. Primary identifications during the period of primary narcissism are processes according to which the infantile psyche is perpetually transformed in its interactions with its primary caregivers. It is these identifications that will be *general and lasting*—that will persist over time, opening up an experience of time that will pervade the development of character by selecting for secondary identifications with regard to what in the meantime have become external objects in the proper sense of the term.

28 *Freud—sublimation and superego*

Responsibility

The origin of the ego ideal is rooted in this primary process of identification with the parents, in which self is other, and in which the investment of libido as care conditions the emergence of the capacity for self-care which will result in the capacity to project a horizon of future possibility that will guide the child into an inspiring sense that there are ideals that are *worth living up to,* by working on the self and by *working things out*. Prior to any specific content assigned to this projected horizon would have to correspond a process of primary idealization in which a future of pure possibility is projected forward. In the context of primary narcissism, this primary idealization, which would be the indistinguishable correlate of primary identification, would be the basis upon which is constituted the primitive possibility of *hope*. Arriving before the registration of *sexual* difference (in that it concerns the parents rather than just the father, as Freud concedes in the supplemental footnote), primary identification as the registration of parental care is the registration of *generational* difference in the act of primary idealization according to which a future horizon of possibility—of life as something to be *lived fully* by *becoming an adult*—is first engendered.

If the infant could articulate this (and it is crucial that it cannot, that this transpires in an element that is anterior to language—at the level of what Christopher Bollas, who I will discuss in Chapter 3, has called "the grammar of our being" (1978, p. 389)), it would arrive in the primitive form of the child's later statement, "When I grow up, I want to be like mommy and daddy." What Freud is giving us to think is how the categories of mommy and daddy—which are the subject of secondary identifications—are conditioned originally by the cultivation of the sense of the want-to-be, which is the conjunction of desire and historical time, beyond the demands for immediate gratification in the *now* of the drives. Despite the fact that Freud will work most of this out in terms of Oedipal relations and secondarily gendered identificatory differences, he is asking us to think at a level that is not only pre-Oedipal, but that would be "prior" to the pre-Oedipal itself. In this way, the originary constitution of hope as future horizon would be the condition of possibility not only of fantasy but also of the dream. In other words, *primary identification* as *primary idealization* is *memory as repetition* having become *future projection*. This is what distinguishes the emergence of desire from out of the drive, in a way that reflects the emergence of the drive from out of the anaclitic relation to the biological instinct.

In the situation of primary narcissism, in which self-care is other-care as *self-as-other-care*, primary idealization, in conjunction with primary identification—the two processes being different but in no way completely distinguishable—constitutes an openness of self and world, or of what will become self and world, in a primitive element of projection of future possibility. This is why Freud can so casually identify ego ideal and superego in a gesture that will not last once he becomes focused on the superego

Freud—sublimation and superego   29

as heir to the Oedipus complex, which is to say as structuring object relations in the course of socialized development. "Superego" indicates the state of this differentiation-become-agency in the form of an injunction as to what one ought *not* to do (Freud 1923, p. 34), while "ego ideal" refers in the text to that aspect of this agency as the inspiration toward what one *ought* to do, so as to *become oneself* by becoming *mature*, which is to say like others who have *already* endured the process of developmental becoming. "One day I will be like mommy and daddy" means that there is a *one day* that is projected forward as a future, a now that is more than just a not-yet-now, and that is capable of organizing behavior and of making efforts at self-discipline forms of self-care as the repetitive transformation of object-libido into narcissistic-libido and back again.[7]

We can distinguish now between what these two terms serve to indicate within the generalized concept of the superego/ego ideal: *Superego* (*Über-Ich*), as what tells us what we *ought not* to do, indicates a form of inner *spatialization* (*Over-*I), in terms of which the ego can judge itself in the constitution of a "higher" moral faculty. *Ego ideal,* as what tells us what we *ought* to do, indicates a form of inner *temporalization* according to which what is on its way to becoming the ego projects itself forward toward a future thereby inaugurating processes of individuation. Superego in this text and from thence forward refers to an agency that spatially oversees and that judges according to a law that, before receiving any content as law, guides, structures and provides for *careful* self-development. Together these agencies of prohibition and future projection, which are *at the same time* both different and yet one and the same, are the psychical bases of hope, which is to say of a sense that life is meaningful and worth fighting to preserve, and as something the child learns to cultivate within itself to an extent determined by its care-giving environment.

These primary idealizing identifications make the child's irreducible helplessness and dependency bearable by registering a *link* which is also a *difference* between the generations, in which the possibility of *becoming* (development) can be internalized, and as the constitution of any position of subjective interiority. Freud consistently links the development of this capacity to the possibility and origin of sublimation, and in such a way that would indicate a process of *primary sublimation* in the relation between self and world, prior to the advent of any experience that would oppose an internal and from an external position, and that would give rise to a psyche that is capable of becoming structured by means of its encounter with a world that is not only an outside:

> We see, then, that the differentiation of the super-ego from the ego is no matter of chance; it represents the most important characteristics of the development both of the individual and of the species; indeed, by giving permanent expression to the influence of the parents it perpetuates the existence of the factors to which is owes its origin. (p. 35)

30 *Freud—sublimation and superego*

This passage should not only be read as making a claim for the importance of the cultivation of civilized morality. What it also describes is the superego as the "permanent" inscription in the psyche of a past that was never lived by the child, the inheritance of an intergenerational past prior to the child's existence that was lived by the parents, and prior to that by the grandparents, and so on. Beyond any kind of moralizing or self-punitive function, the superego (or that aspect of which Freud thinks under the heading of ego ideal) forms the basis for a sense of history, of tradition, of belonging to a community, and for the possibility of finding satisfaction in contributing to the world and to the continuance of tradition and community, even after the passing of my own subjective experience of history (death)—a satisfaction that will be expressed in the basic sense that, regardless as to our finitude and no matter what hardships we endure, life is better than death.

It is in this sense that, with the robust concept of the superego, which emerges from out of thinking idealization, identification and sublimation together, Freud implicitly arrives at a thinking about sublimation that escapes the classical reading of this concept in terms of the production of culturally valued objects, and provides us with the most rigorous (surviving) account of sublimation as a properly metapsychological concept. Although these will be psychical gestures carried out by the ego in relation to the external world, the superego is that to which they first give rise as a differentiation of the ego—as a form of psychic structure—that will thenceforward function as their organizing principle and possibility. The end result of *primary* processes of idealization, identification and sublimation, the superego will be what organizes and directs these processes toward the cultural field at large, and in particular ways that will lead the child through adolescence into the experience of what it means to be a mature, *responsible* adult—someone able to respond to the world.

This also informs Freud's famous portrayal of the superego as the "heir to the Oedipus complex," which again should not be reduced solely to the instantiation of a moral, self-punitive agency. In fact, if we look closely at the passage in which Freud makes this famous statement, and taking into account that so far he has discussed the two terms superego and ego ideal as ultimately part of a larger whole but as articulating two complementary aspects of that whole, it may appear telling that when he makes this claim about the "heir to the Oedipus complex," it is not the term superego he uses, despite the way in which the phrase is typically cited, but the term ego ideal:

> The ego ideal is therefore the heir to the Oedipus complex, and thus it is also the expression of the most powerful impulses and most important libidinal vicissitudes of the id. By setting up this ego ideal, the ego has mastered the Oedipus complex and at the same time placed itself in subjection to the id. Whereas the ego is essentially the representative of the external world, of reality, the super-ego stands in contrast to it is the representative of the internal world, of the id. Conflicts between the ego and the ideal will, as we are now prepared to find, ultimately reflect the

Freud—sublimation and superego 31

contrast between what is real and what is psychical, between the external world and the internal world. (p. 36)

This passage is typically read in terms of the child's submission to the threat of castration and to the father's prohibition of incest in exchange for access to libidinal investments in objects circulating in the world beyond the family, and this is certainly an aspect of what Freud is describing. But another aspect of what he is describing seems to be that the ego ideal, as that aspect of this newly differentiated agency that projects forward a sense of future possibility, expresses "the most powerful impulses and most important libidinal vicissitudes of the id" by transforming those libidinal vicissitudes (drives) into something else, something "higher" or more *sublime*. This transformation would reflect further what Freud had thought as the transformation of narcissistic-libido into object-libido, which would inform the child's developing appreciation of, "the contrast between what is real and what is psychical, between the external world and the internal world." As we saw earlier, such transformation should not be thought in terms of the establishment of a formal opposition; nor, then, should we imagine that any such logic of opposition should uncritically govern our thinking about the relationship between mind and world from a rigorously metapsychological perspective.

This act of transformation would constitute a means of entrance into the socio-cultural field no less than the more familiar account of submitting to the threat of paternal castration; but it would also imply that entrance into this world (that of mature, reasonable adults) is no less a creative act that *founds,* for the individual, an experience of the world as such—an experience that we might compare to Winnicott's (1970) account of the child's experience of both creating and discovering the transitional object (p. 12). Both creating and discovering the world, so as to develop a capacity to *care* about investing in the world in a creative and contributory manner, would be the child's (as well as the adult's) primary and most radical act of sublimation. In other words, ego ideal as "heir to the Oedipus complex" would mean that the child becomes capable of transforming drives into desire.

★★★

As I noted in the introduction to this chapter, many readers, particularly those trained in versions of Freudian theory that predominate in contemporary academic and psychoanalytic training programs, will likely take issue with much of what I have attempted to put forth here. It has again not been my intention to set forth an account of a "true" Freudian thinking, but to provide a creative, careful reading of a series of Freud's texts in order to draw out the possibilities inherent to the concepts of sublimation and of the superego that have gone unnoticed in much of the contemporary psychoanalytic and academic literature. This has been in order to prepare to think through the

32 *Freud—sublimation and superego*

difficulties—clinical and otherwise—that psychoanalysis and the world in which it struggles to situate itself today face, in the chapters that follow.

The capacity to think *for oneself*—to *individuate* oneself—is rooted in the capacity to fantasize, which is always a capacity to *dream* not just of a past but of a *future* that is happening as if it were *now*, while recognizing that it is not, until this fantasized future and the present moment coincide—which will never *actually* happen in any final sense but which must be consistently deferred—due to the efforts of an enlivened sense of self as individuated singularity.

This process, by means of which the drives are organized to become desire, originally by way of the formation of the capacity to dream, where this is understood as essentially dependent upon the infant's interactions with its environment (which is what it remembers when it dreams, without knowing it remembers, like any dreamer), forms the basis for our capacity not only to relate to the world but to participate in it, and in such a way that we are able creatively to contribute to it. This is how we must conceive of sublimation today, in order to think both theoretically and clinically what supports the sense that life is worth its irreducible *struggle* to exist. The marketplace of global consumerism, the insinuation of digital screens at ever younger and more precious levels of development, and the algorithmic control of desire which debases desire to the level of the drives are depriving too many people of this basic sense today that to continue not to think this problem would be purely irresponsible.

Notes

1 Equally decisive here is Strachey's decision to translate *Trieb* as "instinct," which would lead the Anglo-American world into a rabbit hole of misunderstanding Freud as a "biologist of the mind" (Sulloway 1979). This fundamental misunderstanding continues to structure the debate between classical and interpersonal/relational models to this day. Strachey himself acknowledged the confusion his decision might cause, since in Freud's work, he says, the word is "not used here in the sense which seems at the moment to be the most current among biologists" (S.E. XIV, p. 111).

2 We need not take this term in Lacan's sense, but it is important to note how crucial the distinction between drive and desire is for Lacan, especially during the later phase of his teaching, for which this difference becomes foundational (Chapter 4). Furthermore, this distinction between drive and instinct should not be considered specific to Lacan's teaching, but was instead commonplace in continental European psychoanalysis at the time. Cesare Musatti, for instance, who was the most important early translator of Freud into Italian, observed this distinction without any influence from Lacan, and without having consulted Strachey's English translations (Ferruta 2016, p. 19).

3 In addition to megalomania, Freud says, psychosis is defined by a "diversion of their interest from the external world—from people and things" (1914, p. 74). In the papers on "Neurosis and Psychosis" and "The Loss of Reality in Neurosis and Psychosis" from 1924, Freud will concede that this is also true of neurotics, establishing a link between neurosis and psychosis which will ultimately concern the more general question of the relation of mind and reality. This was the question with which he opened the 1911 paper on the "Two Principles," and that would inform much of his thinking for the rest of his career.

Freud—sublimation and superego 33

4 We might claim that Freud anticipated this remark when, at the end of Section II of "On Narcissism," Freud writes, "Parental love, which is so moving and at bottom so childish, is nothing but the parents' narcissism born again, which transformed into object-love, unmistakably reveals its former nature" (1914, p. 91).

5 This is the argument advanced by Loewald (1988), which I will discuss in depth in the next chapter.

6 I cannot proceed without referencing here Janine Chasseguet-Smirgel's classic study, *The Ego Ideal: A Psychoanalytic Essay on the Malady of the Ideal* (1984). Chasseguet-Smirgel's work generally deserves greater attention and reconsideration today, and her concerns in this work in particular—on the superego, the ego ideal and sublimation in the creative process—mirror my own. However, due to her overarching concern throughout her career with the topic of perversion, Chasseguet-Smirgel offers a reading of the cultivation of the ego ideal as a component of the superego primarily in terms of Oedipal development. In this, she follows the letter of Freud's text quite rigorously, and for this reason her study remains essential. She does not, on the whole, however, think what Loewald will call the "microdynamics of memory" (Loewald, 1980, p. 146; see Chapter 2) involved in the construction of the superego. Her treatment of sublimation too, while thoughtful and informative, remains bound to a classical conception with all of its attendant contradictions and difficulties. First published in French in 1975, the book holds up extremely well and remains highly relevant as a work of psychoanalytic scholarship. More than forty-five years later, however, the topic of her analyses requires critical updating for the purpose of accommodating for how the superego and sublimation are to be conceived of in the digital age, as well as for how these "classical" Freudian concepts are to be situated with respect to the contemporary intersubjective and relational turns in the psychoanalytic field.

7 Raoul Vaneigem (2019) has recently articulated this understanding more poetically than I ever could: "The mutation of man into a human being depends on the daily practice of identifying oneself with the will to live" (p. 45).

References

Bollas, C. (1978). "The Aesthetic Moment and the Search for Transformation." *Annual of Psychoanalysis*, 6:385–394.

Brenner, C. (1973). *An Elementary Textbook of Psychoanalysis*. New York: Anchor Books.

Chasseguet-Smirgel, J. (1984). *The Ego Ideal: A Psychoanalytic Essay on the Malady of the Ideal*. Trans. P. Barrows. New York: W.W. Norton and Company.

Ferruta, A. (2016). "Themes and Development of Psychoanalytic Thought in Italy." In: *Reading Italian Psychoanalysis*. Ed. F. Borgogna, A. Luchetti and L. Coe. London: Routledge, pp. 18–35.

Freud, S. (1905). *Three Essays on the Theory of Sexuality*. S.E. VII, pp. 123–246.

Freud, S. (1911). "Formulations on the Two Principles of Mental Functioning.". S.E. XII, pp. 213–226.

Freud, S. (1914). "On Narcissism: An Introduction." S.E. XIV, pp. 67–102.

Freud, S. (1917). "Mouring and Melancholia." S.E. XIV, pp. 237–258.

Freud, S. (1923). *The Ego and the Id*. S.E. XIX, pp. 1–66

Gemes, K. (2009). "Freud and Nietzsche on Sublimation." *Journal of Nietzsche Studies*, 38:38–59.

Kaplan, D.M. (1992). "What Is Sublimated in Sublimation?" *Journal of the American Psychoanalytic Association*, 41:549–570.

Kaufman, W. (2013). *Nietzsche: Philosopher, Psychologist, Antichrist*. Princeton, NJ: Princeton University Press.

34 Freud—sublimation and superego

Laplanche, J. and Pontalis, J.B. (1973). *The Language of Psycho-Analysis*. Trans. D. Nicholson-Smith. New York: W.W. Norton and Company.

Laplanche, J. (1976). *Life and Death in Psychoanalysis*. Trans. J. Mehlman. Baltimore, MD: The Johns Hopkins University Press.

Loewald, H. (1980). *Papers on Psychoanalysis*. New Haven, CT: Yale University Press.

Loewald, H. (1988). *Sublimation*. New Haven, CT: Yale University Press.

Mahler, M., Pine, F. and Bergman, A. (1975). *The Psychological Birth of the Human Infant*. New York: Basic Books.

Sulloway, F.J. (1979). *Freud: Biologist of the Mind*. New York: Basic Books.

Vaneigem, R. (2019). *A Letter to My Children and the Children of the World to Come*. Trans. D. Nicholson-Smith. Oakland, CA: PM Press.

Winnicott, D.W. (1958). "The Capacity to Be Alone." *International Journal of Psycho-Analysis*, 39:416–420.

Winnicott, D.W. (1970). *Playing and Reality*. New York: Routledge.

2 Hans Loewald—between Freud and Heidegger

In *The Question of Lay Analysis* (1926), Freud laments the fact that "in the field of psychology there is, so to speak, no respect and no authority." He writes,

> In that field, everyone can 'run wild' as he chooses. If you raise a question in physics or chemistry, anyone who knows he possesses no 'technical knowledge' will hold his tongue. But if you venture upon a psychological assertion you must be prepared to meet judgments and contradictions from every quarter. In this field, apparently, there is no 'technical knowledge.' Everyone has a mental life, so everyone regards himself as a psychologist. But that strikes me as an inadequate legal title. The story is told of how someone who applied for a post as a children's nurse was asked if she knew how to look after babies. 'Of course,' she replied, 'why, after all, I was a baby once myself.' (p. 192)

Psychology is a field in which everyone deems himself capable of exercising a degree of expertise. Having been a baby, one can assert expertise in child-care. Having a psyche, one can assert a right to speak with expertise about psychology. The search for authority figures in this field is not tempered but exacerbated by this claim that "technical knowledge" is unnecessary. According to an "inadequate legal title," everyone today is granted the *right* to speak as an authority where psychology as a science is concerned.

At the opening of his lecture "On Time and Being" (2002a), Heidegger, in a remarkably similar passage, offers the same lamentation with regard to the status of philosophy today:

> If we were to be shown right now two pictures by Paul Klee, in the original, which he painted in the year of his death—the watercolor "Saints from a Window," and "Death and Fire," tempera on burlap—we should want to stand before them for a long while—and should abandon any claim that they be immediately intelligible.

> If it were possible right now to have Georg Trakl's poem "Septet of Death" recited to us, perhaps even by the poet himself, we should want to

DOI: 10.4324/9781003243878-2

36 *Hans Loewald—between Freud and Heidegger*

> hear it often, and should abandon any claim that it be immediately intelligible.
>
> If Werner Heisenberg right now were to present some of his thoughts in theoretical physics, moving in the direction of the cosmic formula for which he is searching, two or three people in the audience, at most, would be able to follow him, while the rest of us would, without protest, abandon any claim that he be immediately intelligible.
>
> Not so with the thinking that is called philosophy. That thinking is supposed to offer "worldly wisdom" and perhaps even be a "Way to a Blessed Life." But it might be that this kind of thinking is today placed in a position which demands of it reflections that are far removed from any useful, practical wisdom … Here, too, we should then have to abandon any claim to immediate intelligibility. (pp. 1–2)

These passages should not be read as the curmudgeonly complaints of aging patriarchs. Both Freud and Heidegger are attempting to describe a more general cultural shift. Everyone has a mind, so it can be assumed that everyone can be a psychologist. Everyone loves wisdom, so everyone can be assumed to be a philosopher. Efforts to contribute to the tradition of knowledge apparently possess no authority in these fields. Everyone can claim authority; therefore, no effort of thought is required. As a result, there is no thought, and in the absence of knowledge and authority, discourse can "run wild." For both Freud and Heidegger, this trend is not specific to the domains of knowledge under discussion. Psychology and philosophy are only among the first fields that are succumbing to a more general cultural trend. Like the proverbial canaries in a cultural coal mine, they register the pull toward the generalized relativism of anti-intellectual, "postmodern" culture. What will eventually be portrayed as an Enlightenment-based suspicion toward meta-narratives is in fact an either naively or cynically embraced opportunity not to have to do any seriously thoughtful work.

There are, however, significant differences between the two complaints. Freud regrets the denigration of "technical knowledge." The public claim is for a psychological science free of conceptual jargon, one that does not challenge our most basic assumptions about our experience of mind. One should not have to think too much about a science of thinking. Freud pines for the respect accorded to physicists and chemists whose hard work and years of study have earned them the power of causing the uninitiated to hold their tongues. "Technical" here is equivalent to "theoretical," in the sense that theorizing is held to be an abstraction from the immediately accessible, and thus an obfuscation of what should require no effort at advancing one's intelligence or to transform the everyday experience of mind, which Freud had ambitiously attempted to do. The dissolution of authority based on "technical" knowledge in the science of mind is a refusal of knowledge in a claim to generalized expertise.

Hans Loewald—between Freud and Heidegger   37

Heidegger, on the other hand, portrays this same orientation as a *demand* for technical knowledge, one that reduces philosophy to a program for achieving a "Blessed Way of Life." In Heidegger's view, both the humanities and the sciences can still command respect for their authority precisely because they cannot be reduced to practical procedures of counseling. All such procedures respond to a demand for immediate intelligibility, which obviates the time required for intelligent, reflective thought. We would not expect art, poetry or science to be so effortlessly digested, but from philosophy we demand an a priori clarification that renders all mental effort to be an effect of unnecessary abstruseness. For Heidegger, philosophy is in this way quickly assimilated to the demands of consumerism, and this is the harbinger of things to come. The point of philosophy, of thought as such, for Heidegger, is to take time, to linger in the attitude of asking rather than of answering questions: "The point is not to listen to a series of propositions, but rather to follow the movement of showing" (2002a, p. 2).

It could be argued that what Freud and Heidegger are both mourning, each in relation to his own respective domain of expertise, but projecting beyond those domains, is the fact that there is no longer any regard for sublimation. The absence of such regard is concomitant with the decline in such a capacity. For Freud, "technical" knowledge is the result of a capacity to sublimate ordinary acceptance of immediately intelligible knowledge about oneself and about the world. For Heidegger, the demand for immediate intelligibility refuses any effort at sublimation by settling for a "technical" knowledge without thought, where sublimation would be something more akin to the capacity to linger along with the movement of that which shows itself. In a culture that no longer values skill in thinking, sublimation is no longer a concept worth thinking much about. The loss of authority is thus at the same time the loss of the experience of learning by experiencing, of taking time to learn and to develop skill.

Freud might agree with this characterization of his position, but Heidegger most certainly would not. Heidegger would have undoubtedly rejected the very concept of sublimation, and nowhere does it appear in his writings. Raising that which is "lower" into something "higher" does not reflect Heidegger's portrayal of thought, which is not as a Hegelian overcoming or synthesis but as an effort to "step back" (Heidegger 2002b). Phenomenologically conceived, to think is to step back in the sense of taking one's time, leaving aside attempts to succeed in being productive and instead to open oneself up to what reveals itself when an everyday attitude is sufficiently bracketed. For Heidegger, this is the opposite of a "technical" approach that closes itself off to the self-showing of phenomenal experience in favor of the self-centered, narcissistic satisfaction of immediate intelligibility. The very concept of sublimation as a raising up of that which is low unto that which is high is precisely the figure of thought that Heidegger's project had from the beginning sought to challenge. In *What is Called Thinking?* (1976), he had famously insisted that what is scandalous about contemporary thought is that "we are still not thinking" (p. 4).

38 *Hans Loewald—between Freud and Heidegger*

Between Freud's demand for a technically rigorous conceptual approach to the study of mind, and Heidegger's dismissal of immediate intelligibility as a condition for a genuinely philosophical thought, lies Hans Loewald. It is often mentioned that, prior to his medical and analytic training, Loewald had been a student of Heidegger, but surprisingly little has been written about the direct influence that Heidegger quite obviously and demonstrably had on Loewald's thinking about psychoanalysis. In being portrayed as a conservative revolutionary, Loewald is too often reduced to being a "classical" drive theorist who nevertheless carved out a space for object relations in Freudian thought, thereby anticipating the contemporary intersubjective and relational turns (see, for instance, Mitchell 2000). This is a seriously inadequate appreciation of the stakes of Loewald's project, one that fails completely to grasp how Heidegger—whose influence can be read on virtually every page of Loewald's writing—informs Loewald's approach, locating his thought beyond the bounds of a classically metaphysical, intersubjective framework. Without an understanding of Heidegger's contributions to a non-classical thinking about relationality, the truly revolutionary aspects of Loewald's work, and the extent to which these had already anticipated trends in the contemporary literature that are only now beginning to look beyond the relational turn, will continue to go unnoticed.

It is in relation to Loewald's writings on the superego and on sublimation that Heidegger's influence is most recognizable. This chapter will attempt to render explicit that influence in order both to draw out Loewald's still unrecognized radicalism and again to demonstrate why these irreducibly interrelated concepts are worth the effort at retrieving today, despite their largely having fallen out of fashion in the contemporary analytic literature.

Heidegger—primordial relationality

Situating Loewald at the crossroads of his Freudian and Heideggerian commitments requires outlining some of the basic, salient aspects of Heidegger's thinking from Division One of *Being and Time* (1996).

Being and Time famously opens with the attempt to retrieve the question of the meaning of being from the oblivion of what Heidegger calls metaphysics. The first move is to show us that we have forgotten today something of supreme significance—a question that was of fundamental importance in earlier eras: the question of the meaning of being. This is not the same as the question, "What is the meaning of life?" This latter question presumes that life, as a phenomenon beyond a purely biological determination, is possessed of ("has") not meaning but *a* particular meaning, which is to say an explanation that would also constitute a program for how we should live. This question and the assumptions built into it are symptomatic of the forgetting of the question to which Heidegger wants to draw our attention or to retrieve. By asking after the question of the meaning of being, Heidegger is reminding us that existence is an experience of meaningfulness—not that life has *a* meaning but that it is indeterminably meaning*ful*—and that this experience is retrievable if only we are capable of asking after it in the form of a question. "What is the meaning of life?" presumes that we can experience this meaningfulness if we are possessed of the correct answer to the question. Heidegger turns this assumption on its head by indicating that it is only as long as the question remains open, and as long as we remember to ask it, that life remains meaningful.

Being (*Sein*) is obviously what all beings are, but this "are" or this "is" that being itself is not the same "is" that we are used to in our familiar speaking about beings. The "is" of being is not the "is" of a being either definitely or indefinitely specified. Being itself is not a being like any other (the chair, the ocean, the cat), so to state that being itself *is* implicates a different sense of this ordinary, everyday word. From the traditional point of view, the concept of being is the most universal and therefore the most empty and indefinable. Heidegger counters this claim by insisting that being itself is not a being. The fact that we understand a statement as apparently simple as "the book is on the table" without any difficulty reveals that there is a definite if unarticulated pre-comprehension of the nature of the "is." This is the "formal structure of the question of being" (p. 3), which must be worked out.

Every time we use the verb "to be," we presume that everything to which we can apply this verb is accessibly "there." This presumption speaks to that pre-comprehension belonging to the being for which being can become a question. The point of departure for investigating the fact of this pre-comprehension is to interrogate the being that inquires into its being: Da-sein (literally, "there-being"). The radicalization of the question of being that belongs to Da-sein begins by asking: How can Da-sein make itself accessible to itself? One might think that Da-sein, since it is what we *are*—our existence—would be immediately accessible, but this is not the case. In the relation between Da-sein and being, we are furthest from ourselves precisely in being so close.

The way in which this proximity-in-distance that constitutes our pre-comprehension of being is ordinarily concealed or forgotten says something about why Da-sein can only be in a world. The fact that we so readily understand what is meant by the word "is"—without being able to offer a coherent definition of that word when prompted—indicates that it describes something about the way in which human beings, as questioning beings, relate to the world. Even though being (the precise meaning of "am" and "is") is hidden from us, the fact that it's hidden while being accessible at all demonstrates its importance.

There is a temporal implication in all talk about being: "I *am* fine" implicitly means, "I am fine *now*." This sense of time belongs to the pre-comprehension of being that requires articulation:

> time must be brought to light and genuinely grasped as the horizon of every understanding and interpretation of being. For this horizon to

40 *Hans Loewald—between Freud and Heidegger*

> become clear we need an *original explication of time as the horizon of understanding of being, in terms of temporality as the being of Da-sein which understands being.* (p. 15; emphasis in original)

In other words, when I suppose this "now" of the "I am," I am implicated in a pre-ontological understanding of temporality—something I know but that I don't know that I know. The common understanding of time as the succession of past, present and future develops from out of this pre-comprehended complexity of time—from out of an "originary temporality" that does not operate in the ordinary sense of a linear progression from past to present to future.

Time is the possibility of history—there could be no history without time. The extent to which this is obvious is, again, precisely what Heidegger insists needs to be worked through. As the *possibility* of history, time is *historicity*: "historicity means the constitution of being of the 'occurrence' of Da-sein as such" (p. 17). No being, no time and vice versa:

> In its factual being, Da-sein always is as and "what" it already was. Whether explicitly or not, it *is* its past ... Da-sein "is" its past in the manner of *its* being which…on each occasion "occurs" out of its future. In its manner of existing at any given time, and accordingly also with the understanding of being that belongs to it, Da-sein grows into a customary interpretation of itself and grows up in that interpretation. (ibid.; emphases in original)

Thinking the past as coming out of the future involves thinking about time synthetically, as a dynamic relation. This dynamic relationship between past, present and future must exist prior to the ordinary, linear progression of history proper, so that this progression can appear narratively meaningful. The meaningfulness of human existence is temporality as historicity as the possibility of history. Our experience of history depends upon the possibility of temporal relatedness: "This understanding discloses the possibilities of its being and regulates them. Its own past ... does not follow after Da-sein but rather always already goes ahead of it" (p. 18). Da-sein *is* its past, in that its past always already goes ahead of it as something it moves toward. As obscure as this sounds, this is only because we haven't yet worked it out and made its claim explicit. Once we do so, we arrive at an understanding that we have always already understood yet forgotten, perhaps more deeply than anything else, and because it concerns something altogether different from anything else, something familiar but strange.

Heidegger's next step is to argue that, just as Da-sein has this vague pre-comprehension of being, it only exists in a world. It makes sense only as a theoretical abstraction to imagine a human being existing in the absence of any environment, and yet that is exactly what we imply every time we use a metaphysical vocabulary that opposes a subject to a world of objects. The very notion of subjectivity implies embeddedness within a surrounding environment. And yet the vocabulary used to describe this relation insists on separating out these two terms and treating them as if they could be considered in isolation from one another: subject and object, however correlated, stand formally opposed, the one considered "internal" and the other "external," within a general conceptual framework that makes the question of their relatedness appear to be a source of immense theoretical difficulty. Kant had said that the scandal of philosophy was that after so many centuries it had still not accounted for how a subject could be demonstrated to relate fundamentally to a world outside of it. Heidegger countered by saying that the true scandal was that this had even become a problem in the first place.

In order to draw out a more fundamental and intimate relationship between self and environment, Heidegger abandons the metaphysical, oppositional logic of subjects and objects, and introduces instead the vocabulary of Da-sein and world. Da-sein is not what is meant by "self," but at least initially this term is favorable as a comparative form of reference to indicate that what is at issue is something less absolute and less clear than any Cartesian opposition between inner mind and outer world. At an everyday level, this framework is coherent, but when opened up to questioning it doesn't hold up: There can be no subjects without objects, so rather than posit an intrinsic correlation Heidegger asks us to question the very framework that opposes these terms in the first place. We are not opposed to the world in which we live, so there is no question of dialectically "overcoming" this apparent opposition. What is required is an account of how this apparently obvious opposition became naturalized in the first place.

Da-sein is entangled in a world, and as such it is similarly entangled in a historical tradition. But the tradition as it stands itself deprives Da-sein of the possibility of posing the question of its historicity rigorously. Tradition so far has been a history of forgetting, a symptomatic way of the inhering of the trace of historicity:

> The tradition uproots the historicity of Da-sein to such a degree that it only takes an interest in the manifold forms of possible types, directions, and standpoints of philosophizing in the most remote and strangest cultures, and with this interest tries to veil its own groundlessness. (p. 19)

How does the tradition of metaphysics perpetuate concealment through an interpretation of time? By interpreting beings as essentially present, inhering in a very definite and singular mode of time: the "now" (p. 22). The privilege of the present is the hinge according to which a destructuring (*Destruktion*) of tradition and the investigation of historicity in terms of the structures of Da-sein must proceed. What the tradition of metaphysics does is force us to focus on history rather than historicity. If historicity is related to temporality, time itself needs to be rethought so that tradition can be renewed.

42 *Hans Loewald—between Freud and Heidegger*

For Heidegger, phenomenology is the effort at such a rethinking. But Heidegger's version of phenomenology is not that of Brentano or Husserl. Explicating the meaning of phenomenology, he links *logos* and *phenomenon* according to their common Greek root *phainesthai*. Both refer to the event of making manifest, bringing to light (*phos*). To make manifest possibility is to make manifest something *as* the something that it *is* (p. 29). Heidegger stresses the synthetic capacity of what we mean when we use the word "as" to demonstrate that this seemingly innocuous word actually indicates a sophisticated ontological structure intrinsic to being itself. Even in our usual understanding of judgment as predication, there is a synthesis: "The book *is* on the table." Only because we can encounter book and table, only because there is such an encounter can there be a predicative judgment. The encounter precedes the judgment, and this is what it means to be always already in the world, where the world is primarily what Heidegger calls a "totality of relevance" (p. 80). *Logos* isn't just about judgment; it's about the encounter with something *as* something. The structure of synthesis describes the encounter from which the judgment derives. *Logos* is about understanding relatedness: the temporal "as"-structure, which will become increasingly important as *Being and Time* progresses.

For Heidegger, truth is not about the opposition of truth and falsity. Truth as the possibility of any encounter is about unconcealment. Truth is not correspondence (*adequatio*) but unconcealment (*alethea*). Any conception of truth as mediated (representational) relation is symptomatic of the forgetting constitutive of the history of metaphysics. Truth conceived as mediated encounter (i.e., the inner representation by a subject of an outer object) expresses the forgetting of the question of being. This is why Heidegger describes an understanding of truth as the play of concealment and unconcealment. This is a way of thinking truth beyond its determination as correct correlation or correspondence: "because *logos* as *legomenon* [that which lies before us] can also mean what is addressed, as something that has become visible in its relation to something else, in its 'relatedness,' *logos* acquires the meaning of *relation* and *relationship*" (p. 30; emphases in original). This is a relationality prior to *relata*—relations that have yet to do with subjects or objects. Typically we think of relationships as secondary to the pre-constituted beings that enter into such relationships. Heidegger is challenging us to think a kind of relationality that precedes or is anterior to this structure—and in such a way that complicates the ordinary understanding that opposes temporal precedence and spatial anteriority.

Metaphysics forgets or conceals truth as unconcealment. To bring unconcealment out of concealment is something other than uncovering truth as we normally think of it. For Heidegger, this is the task of phenomenology: to describe being as rigorously as possible. Descriptive phenomenology sounds redundant, but it's not like botany: Phenomenology means trying to describe the unmediated encounter which articulates the as-structure (something *as* something).

Where the phenomenological concept of phenomena means unconcealment, we have to get rid of the privative sense of "mere appearance" so that description remains content-free and doesn't presuppose causal relations. This kind of description brings things out into the openness of unconcealment. This is why "phenomenological description is *interpretation*" (p. 33; emphasis in original). We don't normally think of description as interpretation, but rigorous description of being is analysis, not just classification. Phenomenological description is interpretive because it uncovers what is normally concealed, just like in the psychoanalytic sense of interpretation.

Heidegger then arrives at a formula that belongs intimately to the history of metaphysics, which has determined all possible thought: "*The 'essence' of Da-sein lies in its existence*" (p. 40; emphasis in original). "Existence" is typically taken to mean "objective presence," so that "essence" is thought as "whatness": The whatness of something defines its objective presence—its "being here now." Heidegger is pushing us to think beyond this simplistic framework. *Being and Time* is concerned with the possibilities available to Da-sein, not the actuality of its being as subject. Antipathy to the structure of subjectivity marks the vast difference between Heidegger's project and all anthropological concepts of the human.

The modern conception of mind, humanity and science begins with Descartes' *cogito, sum*. Descartes focused on the *cogito* to the exclusion of any reflection on the *sum*. In the positing of the *cogito*, the *sum* is taken to be self-evident. This is a perfect example of the forgetting of the question of being: *Cogito, sum* implicitly indicates that the *cogito* can be excluded from its being and can be looked at in isolation from the world. The subject in this sense is always implicitly rendered as otherworldly and eternal, such that everything is always referred back to it—truth in Descartes, for instance, without which modern science would be inconceivable. As soon as you have the idea of the subject, you have forgotten being. Nothing that describes possibility can be based on this reductionist idea.

What are we doing if we're not thinking in terms of subjects and objects? Who is thinking this and what is this thinking? Heidegger has in effect already answered these difficult questions by the time he begins his attack on the modern Cartesian subject: description as interpretation. What is left when one is no longer thinking in terms of subjects and objects is Da-sein making itself manifest by describing itself phenomenologically—interpreting itself. To think Da-sein as neither subject nor object but as being-in-the-world as what we *are* is "the most radical individuation" (p. 34). Da-sein is not the subject or self; "I" and "you" are not relevant terms in the disclosure of possibility. But Da-sein is still radically *mine*—a process of extreme individuation without subjectivity.

The self considered ontologically or "existentially" will therefore have to be a very different kind of self, since *being* a self cannot be a modality of objective presence: "The who is what maintains itself in the changes through its modes of behavior and experiences as something identical and is, thus, related to this multiplicity" (p. 108). Ontologically there is another way of thinking about the self related to the experience of saying "I" in any meaningful way. This is a thinking about the self as something other than what exists in objective presence, as not just another being like books and plants and cats. Unlike books and plants and cats, Da-sein asks questions about being, interrogating itself in its being as a being. Interrogation of being is not self-reflection but rigorous description of being-in-the-world—something that must be worked through. Being-in must be thought otherwise than as objective presence, as being-with. There is something about the way we are with others that requires as much elucidation as the sense of being-in-the-world: "Being-in is being-with-others" (p. 112).

Just as being-in is being-outside, I is with:

> *Mitda-sein* characterizes the Da-sein of others in that it is freed for a being-with by the world of that being-with. Only because it has the essential structure of being-with, is one's own Da-sein *Mitda-sein* as encounterable by others. (p. 113)

One's own Da-sein—the way in which Da-sein is irreducibly *mine*, but not in any sense subjective—means being-*with*. To be open to the world means to be freed into the relational context of being-with-others. This is again about the *possibility* of relations between people, not about the actuality of interpersonal relationships: "the understanding of others already lies in the understanding of being of Da-sein because its being is being-with ... Knowing oneself is grounded in primordially understanding being-with" (p. 116).

What Heidegger is describing is not a relation *to* others, but a disclosure of others *as* others in the form of being-with as an ontological structure that makes significance or meaning possible. Being-with-others is crucial to the possibility of understanding. This is neither an intersubjective orientation nor does it have anything to do with mutual recognition or reflection—it belongs rather to that which makes cognition in an ordinary sense possible. Heidegger is trying to show how relationality can be thought without reference to consciousness, object relations, or space and time in the ordinary sense of that "within" which we are contained. Space and time are not containing structures but forms of relation. This is what it means to say that being-in is being-with as being-outside, which is what Division One of *Being and Time* attempts to describe: meaning as disclosure or unconcealment as *care* (*Sorge*).

If being-in-the-world is being-outside, this is a structure of opening: "Da-sein is its disclosure" (p. 125). Being-in as being open is the same as understanding the possibility of disclosure—understanding self and world as the same thing. This is the ground for seeing what Heidegger calls possibility. Understanding is not a category of cognition but a kind of "seeing" of openness and possibility. This possibility and the kind of "seeing" in which it consists generally goes unnoticed. The simple seeing which understands the as-structure is a form of interpretation.

Hans Loewald—between Freud and Heidegger 45

This is what *Being and Time* is ultimately about: We do not cognitively "take in" information from the outside world and only then afterward attribute meaning to it. It is only because we can see things as they *are* in a context of relevance that we can then break them down into bits and pieces. Beings are not objects to which we attribute meaning, rather beings *are* meaning, to the extent that Da-sein exists as being-in-the-world and as being-with. Bringing the as-structure into unconcealment through phenomenological description articulates the coincidence of meaning and being. The as-structure as openness can be disruptive, which Heidegger first links to fear and then later, famously, to anxiety (*Angst*). Meaning does not stand "behind" being; ontologically, "ground" is openness. Where meaning is ground it can feel like falling into an abyss. The possibility of meaning is about the terribly frightening thing that world becomes with respect to the as-structure as ontological openness.

If meaning is the possibility of meaning implicit in the as-structure, following Heidegger's argument, then the *there*—the *Da*—of Da-sein is about disclosure. Since Da-sein *is* being-in-the-world, disclosure itself is the *there* of being as possibility. Objects therefore can be said to exist independently of the self, but being does not exist independently of Da-sein: "[T]he '*substance*' of human being is not the spirit as the synthesis of body and soul, but *existence*" (p. 110; emphases in original). "Substance" from Aristotle (*hypokeimenon*—that which supports) to Descartes (*res*—thing) describes a kind of primordial object. For Heidegger, existence is not an object but primordial relationality (being-with). The tradition of metaphysics has allowed being to be thought as substance as a material "thing" that is there in objective presence. In Descartes, this is true of substance in both of its guises: in the univocal concept of matter and space as extension (*res extensa*), and in the idea of the mind as what I am now in the instantaneous transparency of conscious thought (*res cogitans*). The relationship Heidegger articulates between Da-sein and being-in-the-world replaces the concept of substance as object with that of being as relation. The kind of relation Heidegger is describing makes object relations possible. This relationality is *time* as the *possibility* of relation. This sense of time is precisely what marks the limit of the subject/object structure. In Division Two of *Being and Time*, Heidegger will call this, "ecstatic temporality" (§65–68)—being-in-the-world as being-outside-oneself as being-together-with others.

In a subject/object structure, being-in-the-world would imply precisely the opposite of individuation (i.e., a failure to reflect into the space of subjective interiority). But since being-in-the-world is what we *are*, individuation cannot be about abstracting ourselves from our surroundings. At the same time, Heidegger is not describing a subject absorbed in an object—being-in-the-world is not a dedifferentiation (as it is, for example, in psychosis). Heidegger's analysis is always concerned with an ontology of the possible, and possibility always implies a differential element: the as-structure. For Heidegger, this is to be thought in terms of dysphoric affects: anxiety (*Angst*) and uncanniness

46 *Hans Loewald—between Freud and Heidegger*

(*Unheimlichkeit*). Being is always being-outside because being is (*as*) being-in-the-world. This is what relates its possibility to anxiety (about the future—what is not yet), and what makes uncanniness intrinsic to being-in-the-world. Anxiety and uncanniness, on Heidegger's reading, individuate Da-sein to its possibilities. From anxiety and uncanniness, there is a flight toward innerworldly beings, and to the tranquilizing familiarity of objective presence. To be really individuated then one must be put through the crucible of anxiety and uncanniness and not evade being-in-the-world as being-outside-oneself as openness and as meaningful (terrifying) possibility.

Loewald—superego and time

Heidegger's understanding of being-in-the-world as being-with-others as forms of relation that we do not "have" but that we *are* appears in Loewald's writings in the guise of a reworking of Freud's concept of primary narcissism (Loewald 1951). In Loewald's vocabulary, primary narcissism has to do not with the infant emerging from out of a primitive, objectless state in order to encounter an object world waiting there for it, but an originary state in which differential relations pertain that have nothing yet to do with relations between subjects and objects, and in which what analysts call the self is fundamentally outside itself in relation to others—integrated with environment. The "unity" this relation constitutes is *not* unity in a classical sense (as absorption), prior to any form of differential tension. To the contrary, primary narcissism, on Loewald's account, reflects a state of primitive differentiation in which self and other are merged, but in such a way that this merger constitutes a primitive (differential, non-oppositional) form of entanglement in which it makes no sense to speak of a subject in opposition to an object world. For Loewald, primary narcissism is a stage of development in which the internal is not yet distinguished from the external, but what circulates within this state are relations (between the baby's irreducibly present body and the possibility of the absent breast, for example) in which the otherness of the (m)other is constitutively a part of the *process* of the emergence of the infant's sense of self. Winnicott (1960) would make much the same point when he wrote, "There is no such thing as an infant" (p. 587).[1]

It is with "Superego and Time" (1962), however, that the effort implicit in Loewald's writing to integrate Heidegger's ontological ("existential") approach within a Freudian framework is fully articulated. Here it is not a question merely of understanding a primitive developmental stage in implicitly Heideggerian terms, but an effort to think Freudian psychic structure as such in terms that explicitly demonstrate a fundamentally Heideggerian commitment. The title of the essay itself could not announce this more explicitly, even if this announcement would certainly have been lost on his contemporaries, as well as on most of those who continue to speak in Loewald's name today.

The central thesis of the essay is that "psychic structures are temporal in nature" (1980, p. 43). In the opening lines of the essay, Loewald introduces this claim cautiously, if not almost apologetically, as merely "an experiment in thinking." In fact, this argument presents a bold challenge to the deep-seated, if implicit, tendency to think psychic structures as if they were objects arranged spatially (i.e., the superego stands "above" the ego; the ego is conceived of as situated "between" id, superego and external world; etc.). Since this is a tendency to confuse psychic structures with their underlying biological substrates, Loewald's suggestion is that we think temporality as the basic principle of psychic organization. This is not merely to substitute one term for another, but fundamentally to transform what is meant by psychic structure in the process.

Temporality provides the key, for Loewald, to think psychic organization in an "active" sense. The "integrative and differentiating functions of the ego," for instance, can be thought of as psychical activities performed by the ego in its active orientation. There is already a problem here though, of which Loewald is undoubtedly aware: To think the functions of the various psychical structures as essential activities performed by these structures does nothing to challenge the limitations of spatial relation as the organizing principle of the psyche. To think the psyche "actively" is not simply to think in terms of agencies or units that actively relate to one another. This is what psychoanalysis had in fact always done, and despite Freud's insistence on the ego as a differentiated grade of the id, and of the superego likewise with respect to the ego: Id, ego and superego are first conceived of as existing in themselves, and *then* they interact dynamically with one another. This is precisely the classical position that Loewald intends to challenge; for psychic structures to be intrinsically temporal in nature must mean something entirely different.

Rehearsing all of the ways in which a thinking about time informs psychoanalytic theory—memory, regression, fixation, wish-fulfillment, repetition, etc.—Loewald emphasizes the superego, which he identifies with the temporal dimension of the future, as the starting point of his reflections. Rather than think the superego exclusively in terms of its function as punitive agency, Loewald instead attends to that dimension of the superego which we saw Freud, in Chapter 1, subsume under the heading of the ego ideal:

> Insofar as the superego is the agency of inner standards, demands, ideals, hopes and concerns in regard to the ego, the agency of inner rewards and punishments in respect to which the ego experiences contentment or guilt, the superego functions from the viewpoint of a future ego, from the standpoint of the ego's future which is to be reached, is being reached, is being failed or abandoned by the ego. (1980, p. 45)

Conceived as a future ego—or rather, *as* "the ego's future, which is to be reached, *is being reached*"—the superego appears less as an autonomous agency

48 *Hans Loewald—between Freud and Heidegger*

than as a process according to which the ego relates itself to a future that it is capable of making its own. This is not so much an activity performed by the ego as it is a structural condition of the psyche itself, to the extent that it has internalized "standards, demands, ideals, hopes and concerns." To speak of a temporal organization of psychic structure means that this striving—this "is being reached"—is not a psychical effort but a form of structure as relatedness in the ongoing constitution of a future temporal horizon. In that the superego is not some sought after external object but a dimension of "internal" psychic structure itself, this means that the temporally differentiated psyche (in Freud's tripartite model, as Loewald thinks it) is constitutively ahead of or outside itself:

> Only insofar as we are *in advance of ourselves*, conceive of ourselves as potentially more, stronger, better, or as less, weaker, worse than we are at present, can we be said to have a superego. (p. 46; emphasis added)

To be structurally "in advance of oneself" is to be related to hopes, ideals and concerns that either organize the horizon of future possibility or that lead to breakdowns in self-esteem (shame) when such efforts at self-organization fail. To be outside or in advance of oneself, thought from the perspective of a temporally structured register, means to *care* about the future in such a way that prompts me to behave in ways that attempt creatively to realize that future, or to feel disappointed in myself when confronted with the fact that I have squandered my time in the aimless pursuit of listless consumption. In providing me with the sense that I might become "potentially more," the superego is a structure of temporal openness that compels me to individuate myself in relation to a future that is radically *mine*, and this whether I succeed in living up to my ideals or fail to do so. The superego in this sense *is* this "is being reached" as appropriating, organizing and projecting the dimension of the psychic past, which Loewald identifies with the notion of the id:

> The id, if it can be said to represent the inherited past, the degree and quality of organization with which we are born, has a future insofar as we make it ours by acquiring it, by imprinting on it the stamp of ego organization. Insofar as this is an unfinished task, and to the extent to which we experience it as an unfinished, never finished task, our superego is developed. The superego then would represent the past as seen from a future, the id as *to be organized*, whereas the ego proper represents the id as organized at present. The three organizational levels, while representing the three temporal modes, in a being which has memory, creates presence, and anticipates, co-exist, as embodied in the three psychic structures, at the same time that they are successive. And co-existing they communicate with each other, define, delimit, and modify each other. (p. 49; emphasis in original)

Hans Loewald—between Freud and Heidegger 49

By casting temporality as the organizing principle of psychic structure, Loewald has translated into a psychoanalytic register Heidegger's understanding of Da-sein as an ontological structure in which the individual past emerges from out of the future as what Da-sein is always already moving toward. Recall that, for Heidegger, "Da-sein always is as and 'what' it already was. Whether explicitly or not, it *is* its past ... Da-sein 'is' its past in the manner of *its* being which ... on each occasion 'occurs' out of its future" (1996, p. 17; emphases in original). This was the meaning of historicity in Heidegger's account of Da-sein's always already going ahead of ("in advance of") itself, toward its past as future horizon. Possibility is this being-outside-itself, to which Da-sein has always already compared itself, which Loewald is assimilating to the basic function of the superego, *before* it can function as a morally self-punitive agency:

> Considering psychic past and psychic future from a different angle, we can say that the future state of perfection which is the viewpoint of the superego by which we measure, love and hate, judge ourselves and deal with ourselves, recaptures the past state of perfection we are said to remember dimly or carry in us as our heritage and of which we think we see signs and traces in the child's innocence when he is at one with himself and his environment. (Loewald 1980, p. 50)

Where to be at one with oneself is to be at one with one's environment—the basic developmental stage that Loewald had thought in terms of Freud's primary narcissism—this is not to be thought as a static unity or merger, but dynamically as the interactive temporal relatedness that links id, ego and superego in such a way that psychic structure and environment (time) mutually implicate one another: id, ego, superego/past, present, future. Defining, delimiting and modifying one another, Freud's structural agencies are refigured by Loewald in terms of what he will call, in "The Experience of Time" (1972), the "microdynamics of memory," which constitutes a "history-making or time-weaving memorial activity" that is historicity:

> The microdynamics of memory is the microcosmic side of historicity, i.e., of the fact that the individual not only *has* a history which an observer may unravel and describe, but that he *is* history and makes his history by virtue of his memorial activity in which past-present-future are created as mutually interacting modes of time. Psychoanalysis is a method in which this memorial activity, shared by patient and analyst and more or less strongly defended against by the patient, is exercised, reactivated, and promoted. (1980, p. 146; emphases in original)

Here Loewald clarifies, ten years later, how thinking time as the organizational principle of psychic structure allows for a new way of thinking about the therapeutic action of psychoanalysis: integrating mind as memorializing

50   *Hans Loewald—between Freud and Heidegger*

activity with environment as historicity, thereby creating meaning and tradition by fostering integration in the effort to disclose possibility (being-outside or in advance of oneself). This is an analytic rendition of Heidegger's notion of radical individuation in the effort of Da-sein to interpret itself *as* itself, to bring its *there* (*Da*) into unconcealment. This is entirely different from seeking after the objective truths of the past that causally determine our modes of being in the present.

For Heidegger, Da-sein interprets itself in its being as possibility; it does not represent itself in its being as actuality. Interpretation is what Heidegger opposes to the everyday value of representation. To interpret is to open up time—to temporalize time—to disclose an openness that is not spatial but temporal, in such a way that representation cannot be repetition of the same, so that representation is openness and invention, not the recurrence of an anterior present moment (as in the compulsion to repeat intrinsic to the symptom). To do this means to appropriate the past in an authentic (*Eigentlich*) way—to take up a relation to my past, which *cannot be opposed* to the past of tradition and history.[2] In order to appropriate the past which we *are* in an authentic way, this requires, as always for Heidegger, that we retrieve the question of our being. This is implicit in Loewald's thinking about psychoanalysis as "a method in which this memorial activity, shared by patient and analyst and more or less strongly defended against by the patient, is exercised, reactivated, and promoted." The analyst, in this sense, functions as a kind of "superego" intrinsic to the clinical environment itself as a form of disclosure of being-in-the-world as being-with-others.

Ecstatic psychoanalysis

As stated earlier, the concept of sublimation plays no role in Heidegger's thinking. To capitulate to modernity's distribution of the values of the "high" and the "low" in culture is to betray the effort at radical individuation by means of the interpretive disclosure of Da-sein in the retrieval of the question of being.

It is interesting then that Loewald devoted a number of his final years to working on the topic, and that he appears to have considered his essay on the topic his finest work. Did Loewald finally abandon his Heideggerian commitment in his later years, or does his essay on sublimation rather represent his most sophisticated integration of Freud and Heidegger?

Sublimation (1988) opens with an acknowledgment that, for the psychoanalyst, the concept of sublimation "is at once both privileged and suspect" (p. 1)—that it has, as we saw in Chapter 1, presented a number of difficulties and paradoxes that have led to the general abandonment of the concept today. With the fragmentary nature of the text, Loewald makes it all but explicit that his intention is not to resolve these paradoxes, but to demonstrate how the very concept leads psychoanalysis to question some of its most basic assumptions about the relationship between mind and world. It is not so much a question, for Loewald, of integrating a theory of sublimation into the theoretical framework of psychoanalysis, as it is of rethinking that theoretical framework in order to appreciate what sublimation consists in and why continuing to reflect rigorously on this is crucial for the future of the discipline. As he notes in the Preface, writing a book on sublimation is itself an act of sublimation (p. ix), such that to *think* sublimation, which is to say to *write* about sublimation, is to *do* it—what would be called, in certain circles, a performative gesture.

Loewald begins by comparing the ambiguities inherent to the concept to the ambiguities inherent to what it means to speak of "facts" psychoanalytically. Freud had distinguished psychical reality from material reality, but his commitment to scientific materialism left him wavering as to precisely how this distinction was to be understood. Deferring to Kant, Freud had insisted that ultimately, unconscious psychical reality and objective material reality could not be known as "things in themselves," only in terms of our conscious representations, and this presents specific problems when considering the nature of the ego and of the process of sublimation:

> There are a number of indications in Freud's writings, from early to late ones, that the difference between psychic reality (instinct-unconscious) and material reality tends to collapse as one gets closer "to what may be supposed to be the real state of affairs." The status of the ego, and with it the status of sublimation, remains even more enigmatic than that. (Loewald 1988, p. 3)

Given what we have seen so far about Loewald's understanding, thanks to Heidegger's influence, of the limitations of a classical subject/object model, it is easy to appreciate why he is not only invoking but from the outset calling into question all forms of Kantian and post-Kantian critique. From a metapsychological perspective, the enigma of the ego—"and with it the status of sublimation"—is that, according to the Kantian framework (which Freud generally shares), its own status in relation to the question of reality remains unaccountable for. This is not to suggest, in the manner of, say, Lacan, that the ego is illusory. It is rather to indicate that *reality must be thought otherwise than in opposition to illusion*. This would also require a new way of thinking about what we mean in psychoanalysis when we talk about factual truth: "The idea of reality, in the sense of some underlying, absolute, 'objective' truth, has itself become problematic since Freud" (p. 3). It is equally likely that Loewald has Heidegger, as much as Heisenberg, in mind with this remark. His point is that psychoanalysis is a science, but it cannot be a classical science, and if it remains so it will never understand what is implied in the concept of sublimation.

For Loewald, Freud's later drive theory represents an advance over the earlier framework which had opposed the pleasure and reality principles because, with the introduction of the concept of Eros or the life drive, Freud allowed for a

52   *Hans Loewald—between Freud and Heidegger*

pleasure in sustaining rather than discharging tension—a pleasure he linked to rhythm, repetition and time (Freud 1920, p. 8, 22, 28). Recognizing that what is newly introduced in *Beyond the Pleasure Principle* is not the controversial notion of the death instinct but the binding power of Eros, Loewald takes up this novelty as providing a new basis on which to think the concept of sublimation. To posit the primacy of the pleasure principle or death drive in relation to an outside of environmental demand ("reality") assigns sublimation a role only under the heading of defense (albeit "successful" defense). With the introduction of Eros, it is no longer a question of the ego either repressing or discharging libido; it is rather a question of how libidinal energies are *economized*: "a distinction may be made between processes that dam up, countercathect instinctual life and processes that channel and organize it" (1988, p. 5). Unlike repression and discharge, damming up and channeling cannot be thought as opposed to one another, but rather must be thought as modifications of one another, implying a principled motivation to find pleasure in binding or deferring pleasure—which is to say in transforming drive pleasure into something else, according to a kind of pleasure beyond that of the (death) drive. This also implies that defense cannot be thought outside of its relation to the question of psychic structure, as if the one could be conceived of as somehow preceding the other.

Remaining committed to the scientific rigor of the theory of the libido, Loewald will portray sublimation in familiar terms as the transformation of libidinal energies (the drives). But as with his theory of primary narcissism, he will not posit an originally undifferentiated state of these energies in the absence of any kind of articulation. Instead, he will situate the very process of transformation at the heart of the psychical itself: "it is important to realize from the beginning that in psychoanalysis qua developmental theory, the term sublimation implies *transformation* of instincts" (p. 5; emphasis modified). To privilege transformation over opposition is, for Loewald, to think in a more rigorously psychodynamic way. This also accounts for the privilege he accords to the concept of sublimation and why its difficulties need to be worked out:

> If the libido theory taken in this general sense is abandoned—if, let us say, primacy of self, in contrast to the primacy of libido, is stipulated—then the meaning of the concept of sublimation vanishes, to give way, perhaps, to a creationist view of the world. (ibid.)

By "creationist view of the world," Loewald is taking aim at those post-Freudian orientations that posit a rudimentary ego structure present at birth or any variation thereof (Hartmann's "conflict-free ego sphere," for example). This would be to regress from a properly dynamic thinking of primary narcissism (as Loewald sees it) to a classical framework that has since been called into question for its absolute opposition of the subjective and the objective. What Loewald calls "a creationist view of the world" is, in other words, what Heidegger had called metaphysics.

Hans Loewald—between Freud and Heidegger 53

And yet, in rigorously defending the scientificity of the theory of libido, isn't Loewald abandoning the influence of Heidegger entirely? What could seem less "existential" than what Loewald is pushing for? What needs to be understood is that, whereas in earlier essays such as "Ego and Reality" and "Superego and Time," Loewald's main project was solely to bring Heidegger's thinking in *Being and Time* to bear on the insights of the Freudian field, here his effort is equally to use Freudian theory ("psychoanalysis qua developmental thought") to alter certain aspects of the phenomenological effort at an interpretive disclosure of Da-sein. It may be that Heidegger is also ultimately guilty of a "creationist view of the world"—that Da-sein may still be too close to the figure of the subject, unlike the theory of the primacy of the drives. The essay can be read as much as an effort at appropriating Heidegger's project into a psychoanalytic framework, as an effort at using that framework to rethink certain residually metaphysical aspects of Heidegger's project itself.

Sublimation would be absolutely central to something like a psychoanalytic anthropology, in that it attempts to account for "specifically human functions ... which bespeak a complex level of mental functioning ... and which are considered non-pathological" (pp. 7–8). "Freud," Loewald notes, "often thought of sublimation as a capacity—not greatly developed in the majority of people—that is conducive to mental health, if not indispensable for it" (p. 8). If this is the case, then sublimation might be construed as the aim of analytic treatment itself. More broadly, it also indicates that sublimation and the theory of libidinal economy provide a way of thinking about how the channeling of the drives can fail to come about—that we can become *inhuman*, in that our humanity can be *lost*, because what is specifically human is not given but must be *cultivated*. This is where Loewald will ultimately break with Heidegger—by offering up a distinctly Heideggerian theory of sublimation.

Chapter 1 begins with the vapidly platitudinous statement (uncharacteristic for Loewald), "Sublimation is passion transformed" (p. 9). But after rehearsing passages from Freud's study of Leonardo, Loewald immediately begins to make bold and transformative theoretical moves (the key word in the opening sentence, it should be noted, is not "passion" but, "transformed"). Again emphasizing the introduction of Eros as a radical break in Freud's thinking, according to which psychoanalysis must think a certain pleasure in maintaining increasingly sophisticated levels of tension intrinsic to the binding of psychic structure, Loewald demonstrates how Freud in fact thinks sublimation outside classical a framework that opposes the material and the spiritual:

> Freud speaks of the divine and sacred nature of the sexual function and its transference to all newly learned human activities, and of the genitals as the "pride and hope" of the living. Divinities rose out of their basic nature by sublimation, separated-out and exalted elements of sexuality which still remain within its sweep ... So much of the divine and sacred was extracted from sexuality that it fell into disrepute, an "exhausted remnant"

54   *Hans Loewald—between Freud and Heidegger*

no longer containing and evoking the divine. Freud is suggesting that it is a disruption within the full nature or scope of sexuality that leads to increasing disconnection between sexuality and the divine. To the extent that the course of cultural development (of both the race and the individual) leads to sexuality's being emptied of the divine—which thus becomes more and more disembodied—both sexuality and the divine are impoverished. The discontents of civilization include not only the starvation and denigration of instinctual life but, one must conclude, the impoverishment of the divine, of spirituality as well; as it progresses, the disruption of the original oneness of sexuality and the divine deprives both of meaning. It is here that the death instinct shows its silent power. In genuine sublimation, I suggest, that disruption is not dominant, or is overcome. (pp. 11–12)

Sublimation is the disruption of the disruption of the intrinsic entanglement of the material and the spiritual, the sexual and the sublime. Sublimation does not "raise" the coarse and vulgar to a higher place, rather it restores the original unity of these spheres from which the tradition of Western metaphysics has been historically and constitutively in flight: "The 'lowest' and 'highest' are enveloped as one within an original unitary experience; one *is* the other, and later they can stand for one another, the body and its powers a symbol of the godhead, the deity a symbol of the living sexual body" (p. 13; emphasis in original). Sublimation is not a question of deriving "spiritual" experience (in Loewald's terms: primary narcissism, integration of self and environment) from the materiality of the body, but of introducing a cut into the gesture that would separate them in the first place, so as to affirm an identity that is again, and despite Loewald's vocabulary here, not a unity in a classical sense but in which "the one *is* the other."

For Loewald, it is this unity-in-difference that the psychoanalytic act of interpretation is intended to reveal, as the "symbolic *linkage* which constitutes what we call meaning" (p. 13; emphasis in original). Linkage here implies both separation and connection; it is intended to refuse any attempt at reducing the appearance of the "high" to the truth of the "low." A thematics of "raising up," as figured by the tradition of metaphysics from Plato through Christianity to Hegel, thinks sublimation in explicitly spatial terms. By emphasizing the *linkage* that symbolization does not *produce* but that interpretation of the symbolic is intended to *disclose*, Loewald's effort here is perfectly aligned with his earlier efforts to think time as the organizing principle of psychic structure. Recall that, for Heidegger, temporality as historicity is the possibility of symbolic connectedness, as the basis for a narratively meaningful experience of history and tradition. This is why truth must be conceived as the play of concealment and unconcealment, and not as the correct representation of an object by a subject. Loewald is making this exact same claim with regard to sublimation, as the self-interpretive gesture of a temporally organized psyche:

Psychoanalysis, in this view, does not uncover the truth of objective reality behind illusive higher levels of experience (so that the genitals and their power would constitute the true unadorned reality hidden beneath the disguising symbol of a god). Instead, by juxtaposing the two elements of an original unity and emphasizing the one hidden and defended against, psychoanalysis aims at showing their hidden linkage. (p. 13)

Symbolic linking thus does not belong exclusively to the inner psyche but is a concealed dimension of things themselves in the context of a reactivated primary narcissism where self and environment are dynamically or primordially integrated—where the one *is* the other. This argument will be more substantially developed in the later chapters on "Symbolism" and "Illusion," and it will inform Loewald's rigorous examination of Winnicott on the reality of transitional phenomena. Sublimation, on Loewald's account, depends on an effort at bringing into unconcealment or "showing" this reality, which it is the analyst's task to help the patient perform not by substituting an objective reality for subjective truths but by "juxtaposing" or bringing near the patient and the clinical environment as a form of being-in-the-world as being-with. Sublimation as dependent upon the capacity for interpretive disclosure of symbolic *linkages* (sustained separation-connection) would be seeing something *as* something at a more complex level of radical individuation.

By thinking repression as it pertains not to the symbolized but to the link that both separates and connects symbol and symbolized, Loewald manages to avoid the theoretical difficulties that have confounded the history of the concept of sublimation. Rather than depending upon or issuing from a previous act of repression concerning the content of the symbol, Loewald argues that repression concerns rather that which makes symbolization possible in the form of the connecting link that constitutes symbolic experience (consciously or not) by holding together—while differentiating—mnemically associated items of experience:

> Repression, far from bringing symbolism about, disguises symbolism by interfering with the symbolic linkage and hiding the symbolic function of the symbol. Defense is responsible not for creating symbolism, but for disrupting it, disguising it, and distorting it. (p. 54)

As repression is an act of *forgetting*, symbolization is a form of *memorialization*—which could not be said to *oppose* repression, but is still in another sense dependent upon it. Symbolization here is not just the production of symbols, but the "weaving" of the binding-differentiating links that realize a symbolizing sensibility. It is not the "truth" of the symbol that is lost to repression, but the symbolic *function* that is disrupted, distorted, forgotten—preventing the symbol from being seen *as* a symbol. Interpretation, as an effort at lifting repression, is not an effort to indicate an underlying, objective truth (i.e., what the symbol

56 *Hans Loewald—between Freud and Heidegger*

"really means"), but an effort to retrieve an experience of meaning by disclosing something *as* something:

> I have said that the symbol—an object, fantasy, or image, for example— does not cease to be symbolic when repression is lifted. When that occurs the patient in analysis recognizes a meaningful correspondence between the symbol and the symbolized. The symbol becomes a symbol *for him*, whereas before the lifting of repression it had not been. (ibid.; emphasis in original)

To recognize symbolic processes as "meaningful correspondence" is to bring symbolic connections into what Heidegger had called unconcealment—into the symbolic as the *play* of concealment and unconcealment, as something that cannot be reduced to an experience of objective truth when repression is lifted. To say that, as a result, the symbol *becomes* a symbol (something as something) *for* the patient in this way is to say that the analytic process, as an effort to disrupt the disruption of symbolization, is an effort to prepare the ground for *individuation* through disciplinary procedures of *sublimation*. Sublimation, as the *work* of art that inscribes symbols *as* symbols materially, is the radical individuation of a temporally organized psyche, which psychoanalysis as a clinic of interpretation intends to promote.

If it seems that we are taking too many liberties with Heidegger's insights and attributing them to Loewald's argument illegitimately, let us look at the points of divergence between them, in order better to appreciate their intimate proximity. The most obvious difference is, of course, the ubiquitous presence of the body in Loewald's psychoanalytic thinking, which many commentators have been quick to point out is virtually absent in Heidegger. In Chapter 2, Loewald rehearses the theoretical advances Freud had made in the paper on narcissism with the introduction of the distinction between object libido and narcissistic libido. Generalizing the economics of the libido to encompass both self- and other-relatedness, he invokes the consequent conception of psychic structure:

> This is Freud's thought: the "ego as a whole" (the equivalent of Hartmann's self) is held together by libidinal, erotic bonds which in their basic nature are not different from those bonds obtaining in object relations. Indeed, narcissistic and object bonds—once they are differentiated as such—often remain intermingled, or intermingle again, and are strongly colored and influenced by one another; the two "scenes of action" are in *more or less constant interplay*. (1988, p. 19; emphases modified)

The libidinal relations that bind psychic structure so determined are intrinsically "intermingled" with those that constitute not only the relation to the other, but those "inner" relations that constitute the very structure of the other's psyche. Object relations reflect an ontological being-outside-itself of an erotically constituted "intrapsychic" structure, which is at once a form of being-with (again, one *is* the other). Putting together Loewald here on the erotic binding of the psyche with his earlier work on temporality as the principle of psychic organization, we can say that Loewald's major achievement here is to think Heidegger's *ecstatic* temporality as an *erotic* temporality, from the perspective of a rigorously Freudian metapsychology. The concept of the drive, in this instance, offers a way of thinking meticulously about what it means to say that at the level of primary narcissism, self-is-other—where the time of the drive has become the time of the *link* that is disclosed in an act of interpretation that sustains the underlying impact of the symbolic (i.e., meaning as uncanny terror). Sublimation is therefore not only a process by means of which psychic structures come about developmentally, it is also the intended aim of the therapeutic action of an interpretive clinic:

> In this view sublimation comes about by a change of object libido into narcissistic libido, by an internalizing transformation of passion or desire, by transformation of object relations into intrapsychic interactions—once the interpsychic and intrapsychic are differentiated. The universal road to sublimation is, therefore, internalization. Through internalization the character of objects themselves and of object-relations changes. (ibid.)

This "internalizing transformation of passion or desire" is what was indicated in my previous chapter in terms of the transformation of the drives into desire—the binding of the time of the immediate gratification of the drives in the constitution of desire as a *reaching* toward the future that demonstrates the insistence of what Winnicott (1970), in describing transitional phenomena, would call "non-climactic processes" (p. 98; Loewald 1988, p. 24). This is also to say that, again bringing together Loewald's early philosophical concerns with his late metapsychological reflections, there is no sublimation without superego, and vice versa. Unlike Marcuse (1974) and his followers, Loewald sees that the superego must not be done away with or "overcome" but rather *de-pathologized,* both clinically and as a concept.

It is specifically here that Loewald's analytic commitments turn back as a critique of Heidegger's phenomenological ontology. What Loewald's approach allows us to think, what psychoanalysis "qua developmental theory" allows us to think, what Heidegger could not think, is how ecstatic temporality as the structure of Da-sein is not simply a given, but must be cultivated through *technical* procedures of parental *care-giving*. This does not contradict Heidegger's account of Da-sein's "thrownness" (*Geworfenheit*) as its being always-already-in-a-world, but it does indicate that being-with-others always implies hierarchical differences according to which the cultivation of ecstatic temporality must be generationally transmitted. This is what it means to say that historicity itself has a history, both at the ontogenetic and phylogenetic levels. Like the infant whose extensive period of helplessness and dependency

58 Hans Loewald—between Freud and Heidegger

so preoccupied Freud, Da-sein cannot simply individuate (symbolize) itself—it finds itself thrown into a situation of dependency on *those who control symbols* and the histor(icit)y of their meaning. Where this does not appear to be the case is where Heidegger remains haunted by the figure of the Kantian transcendental subject.

Unlike the ecstatic ontological structure of Da-sein, the Freudian psyche has a developmental history (which does not necessarily imply an origin, since this history, by means of identification and internalization, is always already implicated in a history *prior to* individual developmental history, as a history that is *memorialized* but that has not been *lived* in an ordinary sense). The superego, for instance, is not simply there from the beginning, but is constructed and transmitted along generational lines and across generational differences. This means that the superego, as the dimension of futurity—and with it, the capacity for sublimation—*can be irretrievably lost*, again at both the individual and collective levels.

I will return to the global consequences of this possibility in my final chapter, in relation to the question of the future of the psychoanalytic clinic, and in dialogue with Nietzsche and with the philosopher Bernard Stiegler.

Notes

1 Winnicott writes, "Human infants cannot start to *be* except under certain conditions. These conditions are studied below, but they are part of the psychology of the infant. Infants come into *being* differently according to whether the conditions are favourable or unfavourable. At the same time conditions do not determine the infant's potential. This is inherited, and it is legitimate to study this inherited potential of the individual as a separate issue, *provided always that it is accepted that the inherited potential of an infant cannot become an infant unless linked to maternal care*" (1960, p. 589; emphases in original). Winnicott is clearly using the word "being" differently than Heidegger, referring to the infant as a psychological subject and not as an ontological structure. However, in describing the infant's being as conditional upon the *link* to maternal care, by means of which mother and infant form an irreducible *circuit* or *system* of care, Winnicott is thinking the mother-infant relationship in a non-metaphysical way, as prior to any determination of subjects and objects. In the next chapter, we will see how Christopher Bollas (2001) thinks this linking function of what he calls the clinical "Freudian pair" in exactly the same way.

2 A note on the translation: Like Strachey's translation of *Trieb* as "instinct," Macquarrie and Robinson's (1962) influential rendering of *Eigentlichkeit* as "authenticity" misses entirely the meaning of this term in its original German, providing the English-speaking reader with a completely distorted misunderstanding of the author's intention, and in a way that has historically determined his reception in the English-speaking world. Unlike "authenticity," which signifies a recognizable characteristic possessed of a high degree of symbolic value (as in the cultural aesthetics of "coolness," which has nothing whatsoever to do with what Heidegger is describing, and despite Adorno's (2002) attack on Heidegger's alleged "jargon"), *Eigentlichkeit* is meant to indicate something that is radically *mine* (hence, Stambaugh's superior "own-most" (1996)), but not in any way the possession of a subject. Unlike authenticity, *Eigentlichkeit* can never be demonstrated, as what cannot possibly belong to the order of representation, but that founds an experience of world as a "context of relevance" in Da-sein's being-with-others.

References

Adorno, T. (2002). *The Jargon of Authenticity*. New York: Routledge.

Bollas, C. (2001). "Freudian Intersubjectivity." *Psychoanalytic Dialogues*, 11(1): 93–2015.

Freud, S. (1920). *Beyond the Pleasure Principle*. S.E. XVIII, pp. 1–64.

Freud, S. (1926). *The Question of Lay Analysis*. S.E. XX, pp. 177–258.

Heidegger, M. (1962). *Being and Time*. Trans. J. Macquarrie and E. Robinson. London: SCM Press.

Heidegger, M. (1976). *What is Called Thinking?* Trans. J.G. Gray. New York: Harper Perennial.

Heidegger, M. (1996). *Being and Time*. Trans. J. Stambaugh. New York: SUNY Press.

Heidegger, M. (2002a). *On Time and Being*. Trans. J. Stambaugh. Chicago, IL: University of Chicago Press.

Heidegger, M. (2002b). *Identity and Difference*. Trans. J. Stambaugh. Chicago, IL: University of Chicago Press.

Loewald, H. (1951). "Ego and Reality." In: *Papers on Psychoanalysis*. New Haven, CT: Yale University Press.

Loewald, H. (1962). "Superego and Time." In: *Papers on Psychoanalysis*. New Haven, CT: Yale University Press.

Loewald, H. (1972). "The Experience of Time." In: *Papers on Psychoanalysis*. New Haven, CT: Yale University Press.

Loewald, H. (1980). *Papers on Psychoanalysis*. New Haven, CT: Yale University Press.

Loewald, H. (1988). *Sublimation: Inquiries into Theoretical Psychoanalysis*. New Haven, CT: Yale University Press.

Marcuse, H. (1974). *Eros and Civilization: A Philosophical Inquiry into Freud*. New York: Beacon Press.

Mitchell, S. (2000). *Relationality: From Attachment to Intersubjectivity*. New York: Routledge.

Winnicott, D.W. (1960). "The Theory of the Parent-Infant Relationship." *International Journal of Psycho-Analysis*, 41:585–595

Winnicott, D.W. (1970). *Playing and Reality*. New York: Routledge.

3 The fundamental ontology of Christopher Bollas

The title of this chapter is a play on the title of Sarah Nettleton's book, *The Metapsychology of Christopher Bollas* (2017). As with my reading of Loewald, my aim is to demonstrate how Heidegger's temporalized ("fundamental") ontology informs Bollas's approach both to theorizing and to clinical practice. I have previously indicated elsewhere (Russell 2019, pp. 91–92, fn 1) that the philosophical underpinnings of Bollas's work are more sophisticated than the author seems to wish to make explicit, and in excess of that which his general readership might be capable of appreciating. This chapter initially attempts to render that sophistication with sufficient clarity, with reference to a series of Bollas's texts from across his career, but especially the early essays on "The Aesthetic Moment and the Search for Transformation" (1978) and "The Transformational Object" (1979). I subsequently attempt to integrate Bollas's thinking with a thinking about sublimation and the superego—concepts that, unlike so many other Freudian concepts he has rehabilitated, Bollas has never paid much attention to.

Readers are likely to miss the profound extent to which Heidegger and others working on the basis of the Heideggerian critique of metaphysics extensively influence not only Bollas's conceptual vocabulary but also his method of accessing the primitive dimension of clinical and developmental experience to which he has for decades consistently drawn our attention. It is my hope that my efforts at illuminating these connections will not only contribute to a further elaboration of the profundity of Bollas's thinking, but that it will make philosophers typically considered incomprehensible and therefore easily dismissible by clinicians more accessible and worthy of being appreciated for their potential contributions to the exigencies of everyday clinical practice. The clinical implications of Bollas's thinking can be expanded by appreciating the philosophical rigor which his writing works both to develop and to conceal.

Aesthetic temporality

Bollas's early essay "The Aesthetic Moment and the Search for Transformation" (1978) begins with the statement, "The aesthetic experience occurs as

DOI: 10.4324/9781003243878-3

moment" (p. 385). "Moment" immediately appears as a technical term for which the author supplies an explanatory footnote: "I am primarily concerned with moment as an occasion when *time becomes a space* for the subject. We are stopped, held, in reverie, to be released, eventually back into time proper" (ibid., emphasis added). As "time crystallizes into space," he continues, this "actualizes deep rapport between subject and object. The aesthetic moment constitutes this deep rapport between subject and object, and provides the person with a generative illusion of fitting with an object, evoking an existential memory" (ibid.).

Initial readers of the text would have recognized its Winnicottian inheritance immediately, and Bollas himself is quick to acknowledge the influence of Marion Milner on his thinking. Moment as "an occasion when time becomes space" invokes Winnicott's (1970) notion of transitional phenomena; and as something that both *actualizes* and *constitutes* such a space, there is a clear reference to the concept of the transitional object as something that must be both discovered and created by the child, without the logical paradox intrinsic to this experience being indicated and the illusion broken by the caregivers.

The terms of Bollas's argument concerning the aesthetic moment are in fact already contained in the original concept of aesthetics in the Greek sense of *aisthēsis*, which refers to sensory perception in the most general sense. For the Greeks, unlike for a contemporary cognitive paradigm, such perception does not exclude but rather includes both affect and sensation as modes of encountering worldly phenomena. The experience of *aisthēsis* does not concern knowledge as information but truth as the self-showing of phenomenal experience to an integrated, sensual, affective-intellective understanding. Bollas appears aware of this when he describes the experience of the aesthetic moment as a form of *memory* that is,

> existential, as opposed to cognitive, [because] memory is conveyed not through visual or abstract thinking, but through the affects of being. Such moments feel familiar, uncanny, sacred, reverential, and outside cognitive coherence. They are registered through an experience of being, rather than mind, because the epistemology of the aesthetic moment is prior to representational cognition, and speaks that part of us where the experience of rapport with the other was the essence of being. (pp. 385–386)

The word "being" is repeated three times in these sentences ("affects of being," "experience of being," "essence of being"), and again later in the same opening paragraph with reference to "continuity of being," and even an experience of "being-with." Bollas also links this to uncanniness and to thinking as affective, pre-cognitive reverie: "an experience of being, rather than mind." This would suggest that Bollas is not deploying the term "existential" in a casual, pop-philosophical way, but that an informed familiarity with Heidegger's thinking is at work in what he wishes to introduce in thinking *aisthēsis* psychoanalytically, and in using this to conceive of transformation from a properly dynamic register.

62 *Fundamental ontology of Christopher Bollas*

What is "existential, as opposed to cognitive, memory"? And why is the aesthetic moment, in which *time becomes a space* even an experience of memory at all? Bollas does not spell out the answers to these questions but leaves it to the reader's intuition to judge what is at stake. Actualizing a deep rapport between subject and object, the moment of *aisthēsis* functions as a retrieval, not as a psychological or cognitive "taking in":

> Being-with, as dialogue, is the communicating of the infant with the mother, where the mother's task is to provide the infant with an experience of continuity of being. Her handling of the infant's state of being are [sic] prior to the infant's processing his existence through mentation. (p. 386)

Existential recollection is not conscious retrieval but an evocative experience of a memory that, as Freud would say, had never appeared to consciousness in the first place, and therefore can only be reconstructed. The "dialogue" of "being-with" can occur in absolute silence, prior to the advent of what Bollas will call the Word (p. 388) and the introduction of the *in-fans* into language. This a gestural dialogue of holding, feeding, looking, of general attention and care.

Thinking "moment" involves a kind of thinking that is not representational. This is why *aisthēsis* is a question of memory rather than a question of the perception of an objectively present encounter because it involves an experience of reverie outside "time proper": "For the aesthetic experience is not something learned by the adult, but is an existential recollection of an experience where being handled by the maternal aesthetic made thinking irrelevant to survival" (p. 388). Like Freud in his argument that dreaming is a form of thinking, Bollas is asserting that thinking is essentially a form of memory—that memory is not one cognitive function among many (perception, judgment, etc.) but the very essence of all psychical processes.[1] Existential memory implies that existence is fundamentally *temporal*, and in such a way that is prior to the distinction between affect and understanding, as well as the ordinary, everyday distinction between time and space.

Bollas links the becoming-space of time to the existential recollection of the maternal environment, which articulates what he calls the mother's idiom of care—the idiosyncratic, highly singularized form that a particular mother's practices of caretaking unconsciously assume in her relation to the infant, and that will construct an experience of singularity by making *this* infant *her* infant: "The infant's experience of this handling is the first human aesthetic. It is the most profound occasion where the content of the self is formed and transformed by the environment" (p. 386). Immersion in the mother's idiom means that the mother is initially encountered not as object but as environment: "The self is born into the care of a maternal environment" (ibid.). Care is not initially encountered as the activity of a maternal object— environment *is* maternal care as transformational process. This is the situation into which the infant, according to Bollas's ontology, is born or, to use Heidegger's term, thrown.

The aesthetic moment—again, as the becoming-space of time, and the becoming-time of space, through or over the course of which, "the content of the self is formed and transformed"—in Bollas's terms describes the temporality of infantile *aisthēsis*. Bollas's thought of environmental care as existential space-time—what Heidegger calls *leeway* (1996, pp. 336–337), which translates the German *Spielraum*, which would translate literally as *play-space*, the Winnicottian resonance of which should interest Bollas—describes the ongoing play of formation and transformation of the form and content of the infant's emergent self in "dialogue" with the mother, prior to speech and prior to mentation in an ordinary (cognitive) sense. What he calls the "phenomenological reality of the maternal aesthetic" (p. 389)—in which the infant "dwells in the aesthetic moment with a transformational other: the object that captures and places him in a deep spell of the uncanny" (p. 390)—is the encounter with the mother as she *is*, as primordial being-with. This is Loewald's primary narcissism. The evocation of an existential memory of this situation is therefore not the cognitive recall of an experience "in" the past, but a memorializing process that depends upon a psychic structure that is intrinsically temporalizing, in that it is temporalized by a caregiving other: "Transformational-object seeking is an endless memorial search for something in the future that rests in the past" (p. 391). This insight will be the key in allowing us to think, later on in this chapter, what sublimation might mean from Bollas's perspective.

The problem here, however, which Heidegger would be quick to point out, is that despite the transformational process that he describes, Bollas continues to defer to a vocabulary of subject and object—the framework of metaphysics, which is historically traceable to Plato and to Parmenides, and which receives its contemporary determination from Descartes and Kant. The mother as caretaking environment is not "there" in objective presence, and the infant is not "in" this environment like a fish is in a fishbowl, or like a conscious subject experiences itself as "in" space and time. The infant is not a subject in any classical sense, and the mother is not an object. Neither mother nor infant are merely *present* for one another; rather they *temporalize* one another in an element of ongoing repetition: "[The baby] experiences distress and the dissolving of distress through the *apparitional-like presence* of the mother" (pp. 386–387; emphasis added). An apparitional-like presence is not the here and now of objective presence. This is why the question of the aesthetic moment is irreducibly a question of existential *memory*: Not because the adult can only retrieve this experience as "existential" because it is prior to the introduction of language and therefore prior to the organization of cognition proper, but because the infant from the beginning of life *is* a form of existential memorization, one that is temporalized by the mother's idiom as caretaking environment. By attempting to describe this, Bollas introduces not only a Heideggerian vocabulary but also a way of thinking psychoanalytically

64   *Fundamental ontology of Christopher Bollas*

*with*Heidegger, beyond metaphysics. His reliance on the very terms he is inadvertently putting into question makes this fact difficult to access.

In a way that puts him close to Loewald, Bollas emphasizes that maternal caretaking cannot be reduced to some spontaneous human gesture. Environment as maternal care has for each mother-infant couple a *logic* (p. 386) according to which caretaking constitutes a *system* (p. 387)—a logic and system that emerge from out of the repetitive, mechanical aspect of maternal caretaking, as this is conditioned by the mother's response to the periodicity of biological need. There is a technical aspect to this environment from the outset, and this is what constitutes the singularity of the mother's idiom, which as a result will never be identically repeated with each child she raises. The spontaneous gestures of love and affection that the mother expresses are subtended by an idiom (from the Greek *idioumai*—"to appropriate to oneself") that she unconsciously repeats in a singular and singularizing way, providing a fundamental stability to the maternal environment (no matter how unstable) that will cultivate in the infant a rudimentary sense of its capacity to anticipate the future—a future that later the child can also, and as a result, become.

"Our internal world," Bollas writes, "is transformed by the mother's unconscious desire into a primary theme of being with mother, that will *print* all future ways of being with the other" (p. 389; emphasis added). Like some primordial or ontological machine press, the mother-infant relationship, as environmental/existential space-time, imprints ways of being on the infant that will determine her future horizon (this is what Bollas (1992) will later call "being a character").[2] Perhaps this is why, like Freud (1919) with respect to mechanical dolls that appear lifelike, he invokes the experience of the uncanny. At no point in "The Aesthetic Moment" does Bollas ever justify why he associates existential memory with uncanniness, beyond its appearing as a general nod to Heidegger. But a remark from the follow-up paper on "The Transformational Object" (Bollas 1979), to be considered in the next section, indicates that Bollas is quite clear on this point. There he writes that transformational experiences or aesthetic moments

> are less noteworthy as transformational accomplishments than they are for their uncanny quality: the sense of being reminded of something never cognitively apprehended, but existentially known, *the memory of the ontogenetic process*, rather than thought or fantasies that occur once the self is established. (pp. 98–99; emphasis added)

An ontogenetic process is an individuating process—a process through or by means of which the individual comes into being *as* an individual. This can always only be remembered because while it is occurring it is never simply occurring in the present—hence it can only be known "existentially," which is to say, remembered. But there are no *contents* to this type of memory—as memory of a developmental, individuating process, such memory is rather aesthetic (as the "moment" of *aisthēsis*). Just as for Heidegger in *Being and*

Time, uncanniness is linked, for Bollas, to this "existential" or ontological memory as repetition, which would then be haunted by the unconscious caregiving techniques of the "apparitional-like mother."

As system and as logic, this transformational imprinting of the idiom of maternal care—anterior to speech, before the advent of language in the infant's subjective experience properly so determined as a result—constitutes what Bollas calls "the grammar of our being" (p. 389). A grammar or writing (printing) prior to speech would seem to be an unusual, paradoxical thought. In *Psychoanalysis and Deconstruction: Freud's Psychic Apparatus* (2019), I indicated that Bollas's conceptual terminology often (very often, in fact) betrays the influence of Derrida on his thinking. Distinctly Derridean terms such as "trace," "deconstruction" and "dissemination" are scattered throughout Bollas's writings from the earliest to the most recent.[3] When Bollas describes the articulation of a "grammar of being" prior to language as speech, he demonstrates more than a passing familiarity with Derridean terms.

In *Of Grammatology* (1976), Derrida had offered precisely this thought of a writing prior to speech, in order both to appropriate and to critique Heidegger's efforts at a retrieval of the question of being in relation, rather than in opposition, to the question of *technics* as the question of the *production* of symbols (p. 8). This thought continues to confound most readers of *Of Grammatology*, especially those who still think it is somehow an effort to outline a science of writing, as well as those who either denounce or celebrate it as a literary text without philosophical rigor.

Bollas, on the other hand, has (at least intuitively) grasped Derrida's point rather well: To posit a kind of writing before language is to delimit a pre-linguistic domain that intrinsically complicates what it means to speak of a "before" and an "after" in an ordinary, non-relational way; access to this area of experience requires technical procedures, not only the poetizing reverie of which Heidegger was so fond. And this is because—as we saw Loewald suggesting, extending Heidegger by integrating the phenomenological analysis of Da-sein with psychoanalytic insights into the evolution of psychic structure—historicity itself has a history. The sense of a past that one passes on and that holds one outside oneself toward the future is locally and generationally inscribed, like an idiom, and so must be *inherited*:

> Creativity includes the aesthetic and the thematic. The thematic will print the subject's fantasies, reflecting his own use of the aesthetic frame that contains the thematic. Although the thematic reflects the subject's *inheritance of the aesthetic frame*, it becomes the idiomatic discourse of the internal world. (pp. 393–394; emphasis added).

As uncanny—beyond or before the opposition of the technical and the spontaneous—the play-space of maternal, environmental care, as what culti-vates care-taking and care-giving relations to self and other—and to self-as-other—would be an instance of the forming and transforming process that is

66   *Fundamental ontology of Christopher Bollas*

known in Derridean terms as *grammatization* (a concept to which I will return in Chapter 5).

This would also be true of the analytic process as Bollas conceives it: "the technique of psychoanalysis is primarily an aesthetics of care" (p. 393). What this means will be the topic of the paper which follows immediately after "The Aesthetic Moment and the Search for Transformation," almost as a companion piece: "The Transformational Object" (Bollas 1979). This essay, to which we will now turn, without yet abandoning further commentary on "The Aesthetic Moment," allows us to appreciate in greater depth why Bollas's contributions have from the outset been not just conceptually sophisticated but clinically revolutionary, and to an extent that even his most committed readership seems not yet to have grasped. In the final section of this chapter, I will return, via Loewald, to the question of sublimation and of the superego as they pertain, though the lens of Bollas's writing, in which these terms rarely if ever appear, both to individual development and to the practice of an interpretive clinic.

The transformational process—maternal environmental care

"The Transformational Object" bears with it both the most radical insights of "The Aesthetic Moment and the Search for Transformation" and its failures in not fully thinking through the problem of metaphysics in the effort to portray the time-space of maternal care as relational environment. Bollas again takes up the effort to outline how, "the mother both sustains the infant's life and transmits to the infant, through her own particular idiom of mothering, an aesthetic of being that becomes a feature of the infant's self" (1979, p. 97). This *transmission* is one that *transforms*—so again it is not a question of a subject modally affecting an already fully constituted object: "as the infant's 'other' self, the mother continuously *transforms* the infant's internal and external environment" (p. 97; emphasis in original). Such transformation indicates the distribution of the internal and the external from out of what consists in the mother's original function as what Winnicott (1958) had called a "total environment," in terms of which the ordinary opposition between the internal and the external cannot hold. To say that this opposition cannot hold is another way of indicating what Bollas had meant when he had described moment in terms of time becoming space.

Because the system of maternal care provides a total environment—an "ecology" (Bollas 1979, p. 98), which is to say a systemic eco-logic that is registered or inscribed (printed, written) ontologically as "an aesthetic of being that becomes a feature of the infant's self"—in which time becomes space as the function of continuous transformation of the infant's emergent self, Bollas writes, "the mother is less identifiable as an object than as a *process* that is identified with cumulative internal and external gratifications" (p. 97; emphasis in original). The mother as transformational object is thus transformational precisely to the extent that she is *not* experienced by the infant as an object in the ordinary sense. The mother is not an object but a process, and in such a way that escapes all classical thinking in terms of cognitive subject/object dichotomies: "the first object is 'known' not by cognizing it into an object representation, but known as a *recurrent* experience of being—a kind of existential as opposed to representational knowing" (ibid.; emphasis added). The recurrent—repetitive— function of the maternal object is what makes the maternal object-process an ecologically *total* environment, in which time continuously transitions into and becomes space in the imprinting of the mother's idiom, allowing for the infant's emergent sense of self to be defined within the context of the mother's technical frame *qua* care, and to elaborate itself historically in "an endless search for something in the future that rests in the past" (1978, p. 391). This is the "existential" situation to which Bollas wishes to draw our attention—one in which the correlational representation of an object by a primarily cognitive subject is precisely not at issue:

> As the mother integrates the infant's being (instinctual, cognitive, affective, environmental) the rhythms of this process, from unintegration(s) to integration(s), informs the nature of the 'object' relation rather than the qualities of the object *qua* object. The mother is not yet identified as an object but is experienced as a process of transformation …
> (1979, p. 97)

When Bollas writes here that, "The mother is not yet identified as an object but is experienced as a process of transformation," he should not be read as stating that the infant *fails* to perceive the mother objectively, but that again at a fundamental level—that of "the grammar of our being"—the mother *is* a process of transformation, and that it is *as* a process and not merely as an object that transformation is sought after. Bollas's continued deference to the categories of subject and object again demonstrates both the irreducible insistence and the inevitable limits of this classical framework in the effort to think of maternal environment as primordial relationality. The passage continues:

> this feature remains in the trace of this object-seeking in adult life, where I believe the object is sought for its function as signifier of the process of transformation of being. Thus, in adult life, the quest is not to possess the object; it is sought in order to surrender to it as a process that alters the self, where the subject-as-supplicant now feels himself to be the recipient of enviro-somatic caring, identified with the metamorphoses of the self. As it is an identification that begins before the mother is cognized as an object, it is not an object relation that emerges from desire, but from a kind of proto-perceptual identification of the object with its active feature—the object as enviro-somatic transformer of the subject …
> (pp. 97–98)

68   *Fundamental ontology of Christopher Bollas*

Seeking out experiences of transformation—entering into an analysis, for example, or falling in love, or creating artistically, or becoming intoxicated—is an effort to retrieve an experience of enviro-somatic caregiving. As Bollas goes on to describe, although "the quest is not to possess the object," this is precisely what happens in certain seemingly intractable forms of psychopathology: The experiential process of transformation is sought after in the reductive, cognitive form of a static object, allowing it to function not like a process of creativity but like a source of addiction. This is precisely what the marketplace of global consumerism exploits today: "We know that the advertising world makes its living on the *trace* of this object; as the advertised product usually promises to alter the subject's external environment and thus change internal mood" (p. 98; emphasis in original).

The insight that transformation is what is being fundamentally sought after, as the existential memory retrieval of enviro-somatic caregiving, allows Bollas to think a primitive structure of the self that is prior to the cognizing of things as "outside," in objective presence. This structure is what Bollas calls here "a kind of proto-perceptual identification of the object with its active feature," and later "perceptual identification" (p. 102). Identifying the object with its active feature means experiencing a process. This is not about object relations but about what makes object relations possible, as Bollas attempts to make clear. In a much later paper on "Perceptive identification" (Bollas 2006), he will again attempt to clarify this point by distinguishing the concept from that of projective identification, and not as its opposite but as belonging to another register entirely:

> If projective identification gets inside the other, perceptive identification *stands outside* to perceive the other. The term "identification" means quite different things for each concept. In projective identification it means identifying with the object; in perceptive identification it means perceiving the identity of the object. (p. 716; emphasis added)

"Perceiving the identity of the object" is "identification of the object with its active feature." This is not an objective perceiving that reveals the underlying truth of the object's identity, as formally distinct from the subjective self—it is not a question of appreciating "the otherness of the other" in the way that this is often described in postmodern cultural studies. To identify the object with its active feature is to experience it as a process and precisely not as an object—as transformational (temporalizing), caretaking environment, which is not an environment we are "in" in an ordinary sense. This is a different kind of seeing or perceiving, one that requires *standing outside* oneself.

> Perceptive identification is not equivalent to "taking in" the object. Our use of the concept of introjective identification could err in the same way as seeing perceptive identification as a form of projection. It does not have to do with either putting something into or taking

Fundamental ontology of Christopher Bollas 69

something from the object. *It is a matter of seeing the qualities of the object.* (p. 719; emphasis added)

There is no mistaking at this point the fact that this is precisely what Heidegger had described in terms of Da-sein's ecstatic openness—being-outside-itself as being-always-already-in-a-world as being-with-others—as the temporalization of time which both separates out and holds together dynamically future, past and present. By "seeing the qualities of the object" in standing outside oneself, Bollas means seeing something *as* something: the simple seeing which understands the as-structure, and which is a form of interpretation; being-in as being open as understanding the possibility of disclosure—experiencing oneself and the world as the same thing—and as the ground for seeing possibility; existential memory as ultimately or originally a kind of "seeing" of openness and possibility. This is the kind of seeing intrinsic to both perception and understanding (i.e., "I see what you mean") that must precede their being split apart into separate cognitive functions, divorced from affect or mood as the domain of access to objective truth—the simple seeing that is *aisthēsis* as phenomenological disclosure, in a "moment" of transformation that cannot be figured in terms of a metaphysics of objective presence.

The ecology of the frame—unconscious creativity

The true revelation of Bollas's work is not his proximity to Heidegger, as I have sketched this so far, but the fact that here is a psychoanalyst from the English-speaking world who seems actually to have read Freud. Instead of building his thinking on reductive, textbook versions of Freudian thought that see only in Freud's writings a biologistic, "one person psychology," and instead of returning to Freud's texts in order to impose upon them theoretical frameworks for the purpose of turning Freud into a thinker he was not (Lacan), Bollas pays close attention to Freud's writings in order to draw out essential and novel insights that do not always accord with the image of Freudian thought that we typically inherit. "Freud," it should be noted, does not name a coherent body of conceptual discourse without flagrant internal contradictions. If we are looking to Freud for a model of consistent, logical thinking, we are barking up the wrong tree. One of Bollas's greatest talents as a reader is his capacity to draw out aspects of Freud's thinking that not only disabuse us of the fantasy that his thinking was monolithic but that demonstrate how Freud's thinking contains elements that already anticipated contemporary "advancements" in the psychoanalytic field, and that point in a direction well beyond them.

This is most evident in Bollas's approach to the topic of Freud's clinical method, and what this method suggests about certain neglected or misinterpreted aspects of his theories of mind. Bollas's efforts to rehabilitate the meaning of the practices of free association and evenly suspended or hovering attention demonstrate that, contrary to the widespread belief among both

70   *Fundamental ontology of Christopher Bollas*

analysts and patients today that psychoanalysis is merely what happens spontaneously when one goes to an office to speak to a psychoanalyst, Freudian psychoanalysis actually consists in a very specific set of techniques: the patient attending sessions with a high degree of frequency, for an unspecified and unpredictably open-ended length of time, lying on the couch, speaking without exercising self-censorship or judgment, while the analyst, similarly withholding judgment about what the patient "really means" in what he says, maintains a trance-like, spellbound state of freely floating attention that allows her to "simply listen" (Freud 1912, p. 112), both to the patient's speech and to material evoked by her own unconscious.[4]

Bollas's notion of the *Freudian pair*—the patient free associating, in relation to an analyst who floats in an element of simple listening—has nothing whatsoever to do with what is widely referred to as the "analytic dyad." The pair at issue is not that of an intersubjective relationship, at least not in the context of a genuinely Freudian practice when this is underway in the course of a clinical session. What is paired or *linked* for Bollas, in contrast to models of intersubjectivity, are not two subjects but two *functions*: "Psychoanalysis can be said to be taking place if two functions are linked—the analysand's free associations and the psychoanalyst's evenly suspended attentiveness" (Bollas 2001, p. 93). As in Freud's (1912) analogy that would compare the unconscious to the mechanism of the telephone, the link established by the exercise of these functions is the link between the unconscious of the patient and that of the analyst. The technical procedures that comprise the Freudian pair were designed to facilitate and to amplify the experience of unconscious communication.

Bollas recognizes that the very notion—and it is a strange one, both in an allegedly "Freudian" context and well beyond—of unconscious communication, as this is articulated in Freud's technical recommendations, indicates an unconscious beyond that of the repressed about which Freud had largely theorized: "This unconscious is neither the repressed unconscious nor the id" (2001, p. 95). A *communicative* unconscious is primarily *receptive*, as Bollas demonstrates, leading us to a way of thinking alternatively not only about the Freudian unconscious but about Freudian practice. This practice consists in an effort to *link functions* that are able to enter into a specific kind of relationship that again has nothing to do with but is already in advance of classical models of intersubjectivity or relationality: "Freud invented a new form for thinking and a unique style of relating when he established these two mental positions" (2001, p. 94). What is new in this form of thinking is that neither function engaged in such a way consists in any effort at reflection—the Freudian pair *thinks non-reflectively*, and in ways that can only be done *together*, in the pairing of functions that is the clinical frame, such that thinking becomes not a representational thinking *about* but a constitutively relational thinking *with,* which is to say *between* (cf. Momigliano 2016, p. 349). In the pairing of these functions, the patient's task

Fundamental ontology of Christopher Bollas 71

was to report the irrelevant, which would ultimately, Freud believed, prove to be more significant than the patient's darkest secrets. The psychoanalyst was to assume a meditative frame of mind, more like the practitioners of Zen Buddhism than doctors of medicine. (ibid.)

The trance-like frame of mind that Freud recommends is not a purely psychological state—it merges with and participates in the construction of the analytic frame itself. That is, when, "The Freudian analyst contributes a frame of mind, a meditative *quiet* that evokes and supports the analysand's free associations, object relations, and character moves" (ibid.; emphasis added), he or she provides a total environment. Freud's theories aside, the analytic frame is intrinsically intended to provide a process of maternal care.

Reis (2020) has recently drawn attention to the distinction, implicit in Bollas's thinking here, between *quiet* and *silence*:

> In psychoanalysis, silence is often thought of as the absence of speaking, conceptualized with reference to the analyst's technique or what is repressed or withheld by the patient. I would say quiet is a more expansive term, associated with lived experience in the psychoanalytic relationship between patient and analyst—i.e., thoughtfulness. (p. 73)

Although the distinction Reis goes on to posit on this basis between practice and technique seems to me highly questionable, and not in line with either Bollas's or Freud's thinking, his point is extremely well taken: silence implies withdrawal, absence and lack; quiet implies support for processes of symbolization—*prior* to speech, or as what makes symbolization in an ordinary sense possible. This is what Heidegger had called ground as openness.

The analyst's frame of mind is not merely an activity undertaken by one member of a dyadic pair in response to the other's efforts at free association; the analyst's neutrality[5] introduces rather a function of mind-as-environment— a *psychecology*—in which the floating analyst merges with the patient's experience of the frame in a way that not only holds or contains, but that supports while drawing the patient's mind outside of itself, and not into a space of intersubjective recognition but, on the contrary, into the time of radically individuated solitude:

> We might think of Winnicott's model of the way a mother facilitates the infant's creativity. The child can articulate his or her own idiom by playing alone in the presence of the mother. The Freudian analysand can talk freely in a type of *solitude*, yet entirely contingent on the supportive presence of the psychoanalyst. (Bollas 2001, p. 94; emphasis added)

On the basis of Reis's distinction between silence and quiet, perhaps we can make a distinction between *isolation* and what Bollas refers to here as *solitude*. Isolation can be said to imply that the individual is alone in the absence of

72   *Fundamental ontology of Christopher Bollas*

others, even when others may be present. Solitude, as Bollas describes it, as "entirely contingent on the supportive presence of the analyst," would be more akin to a kind of being-with, yet one not necessarily "in" objective presence and therefore not intersubjective in the strict sense of the term. This would be the "separation without separation" that cultivates what Winnicott (1958) had called "the capacity to be alone," and which emerges from out of the infant's being allowed "just to lie back and float" (Winnicott 1973, p. 28).

The technical frame of the method that unconsciously links, so as to constitute, the Freudian pair, in the quiet and solitude of the analyst's supportive yet non-objective ("apparitional-like") presence, would be a floatation device in this sense—a technology that allows the mind to stand outside itself in the buoyancy of unconscious receptive communication. This is, again, an effort to access what subtends all human relations but that generally remains concealed. Without this "aesthetic" background, intersubjective human communication would resemble nothing more than communication between insects. For Bollas, the Freudian method is implicitly designed to amplify this form of ordinary though generally overlooked or forgotten background, such that unconscious engagement can become the possibility for a therapeutic, transformative experience. This possibility must somehow be prior to intersubjectivity in a classical, metaphysical sense:

> We may conclude, therefore, that all human relations involve a deep intersubjectivity. And, above all other theorists, it was Freud who invented a relational space for the informative processing of this intersubjectivity. (p. 99)

This conclusion concerning a Freudian intersubjectivity should appear in no way astonishing. The real insight here is that of the analytic frame conceived as a *relational space* for the *informative processing* of intersubjectivity. Clearly, by "relational space" Bollas does not (or does not only) mean the room "in" which the Freudian pair meet, to *then* engage in an ordinary intersubjective relationship—a mundane office space, essentially no different from corporate office space, and having nothing yet to do with an analytic frame, including or especially that aspect provided by the analyst's *frame of mind*. Bollas is describing not a space of relation, but space *as* relation, in the way that Heidegger had described Da-sein's ecstatic being-outside-itself as being-in-a-world as being-with-others. This is not a space "in" which the analytic process occurs; it is the space of the frame-as-relation as an effect of mind-as-environment or what Bollas calls the analytic ecology (1978, p. 98).

Relational space facilitates *informative processing*. The almost comically cognitivist ring to this term risks making it sound as if Bollas is describing the analyst and analysand "processing information" about one another in the manner of some kind of digital interface, in which data is exchanged and broken down into units of subjective meaning. He is instead describing an

Fundamental ontology of Christopher Bollas 73

in-formative experience of the unconscious of the other in the context of the unconscious communication of the Freudian pair, which,

> returns mental contents to consciousness as part of the psychoanalyst's unconscious communication with his patient, and it reflects the unconscious creativity of the ego. The psychoanalyst is being composed by and is in turn composing the patient's material. (2001, p. 96)

In-forming one another, which is to say shaping and cultivating one another, through an unconscious communication that is not the transfer of information from one subjective interiority to another, but a mutually transformative, in-formative engagement, the Freudian pair (as *linked functions*) is a relationship between positions of radical solitude that are at the same time a standing-outside-oneself as being-with. This is why the in-formative requires *processing*—not processing as breaking down and digesting bits of information, but processing in the sense of an *analytic process*: time. Where relational space *is* in-formative process—that is, where and when time becomes a space, in what Bollas called the aesthetic moment—the analytic *mind-frame* performs a (trans) formative procedure across linked (open) functions. This can occur—as a kind of writing before speech, or as a *grammatization* of being—in the elements of *quiet* and *solitude,* even eventually (over time) when analyst and analysand are no longer in the room together, and thus remain "apparitional-like" to one another, but *there.*

This is why psychoanalysis, for Bollas, is intrinsically creative—in a sense that is not meant to be taken lightly or metaphorically—even though it might not necessarily appear "productive," these terms being generally conflated today:

> Analysand and psychoanalyst eventually come to realize that sessions "wasted" are far better than sessions falsely exploited simply to organize them into some theme or another, as they are lacking in that kind of inspiration that comes only from unconscious creativity. (p. 100)

Bollas's vocabulary here is stylistically flimsy, but he is describing something incredibly sophisticated. Unconscious creativity, in the sense Bollas describes, is not a naive celebratory event of imagination; it is *creative* in a quasi-material (or "quasi-transcendental" (Gasché 1986)) sense, as the in-forming of a receptive unconscious. In other words, unconscious creativity *is* unconscious receptivity—this is why Bollas consistently prioritizes the question (in both senses of the genitive) of Freud's method, which is formally indistinguishable from the frame and from the pair:

> the method has implications more wide-ranging than the already impressive accomplishment of rendering unconscious ideas to consciousness: it actually develops the patient's and the psychoanalyst's capabilities.

74   *Fundamental ontology of Christopher Bollas*

> This ... is *a new form of creativity fostered only in the psychoanalytic space.* (2002, p. 14; emphasis added)

This creativity is unconscious in-formation over time, which impacts the patient and analyst alike, though in singularly different ways. Surprisingly (or perhaps not), Bollas describes this in terms of *disclosure*: "The psychoanalyst's effect on the analysand is a form of self-disclosure ... [W]hat is disclosed is the idiom of the psychoanalyst's unconscious creativity itself" (2001, p. 98). Does this imply that the analyst's interpretations (which would include his quietness and solitude, and which cause minds to resonate by means of what he calls the "echo" (Bollas 2001, p. 96; 2002, pp. 30–32)) disclose the analyst's person to the patient, or does the analyst's effect on the patient consist in the patient himself being disclosed? If we take the term again as an indication of the influence of Heidegger on Bollas's thinking, the answer is: *both*. But this again has nothing at all to do with personal identity or subjectivity. Disclosure (for Heidegger: bringing into unconcealment—i.e., seeing something *as* something) is what Bollas is calling unconscious communication—something other than but not unrelated to information transfer or telepathy in a banal sense (Bollas 1978, p. 103). What Bollas calls relational space as in-formative processing is frame-as-relation as mind-as-environment—an *ecology* of meaning and significance, which Heidegger had called *world*, and according to which *in*-formation is always *trans*-formation or trans-*substantiation*.

Bollas is, of course, refining and providing a meticulous analysis of what Winnicott had called transitional or potential space (as the space-time of possibility). Recall that, as we saw in Chapter 2, Loewald had attempted to do precisely the same thing, connecting this to Freud's concept of primary narcissism and to the disclosure of the link between elements that constitutes symbolic meaning. This also involved a kind of unconscious creativity as unconscious receptivity: internalization. Internalization, for Loewald, was linked to the question of the superego and to the opening of time as future horizon, and to sublimation as ego formation or as psychic structuralization. This is creative in the sense that what is created *is* the mind *by the mind itself*—in solitude, with others who are essentially apparitional, which is to say memorialized. This is what Heidegger had called radical individuation, which does not flee anxiety and uncanny terror in the face of ontological ground as openness.

★★★

At this point, a response is due to those readers who likely from the outset of this chapter have been troubled by the question as to whether or not Bollas has ever *actually* read Heidegger or Derrida. It can be stated explicitly, and according to the logic of Bollas's own thinking, that whether or not he has ever actually read them (I have no idea) is ultimately irrelevant here: Bollas's work is in-formed by these thinkers, and bears their traces. Like Loewald, he

Fundamental ontology of Christopher Bollas 75

perceives in Freudian theory and practice (which are often dissociable, but for both Bollas and Loewald must be thought *together*[6]) an "existential" or ontological dimension that concerns not the contents of the patient's unconscious conceived as a container of buried psychological truths, but the ways in which analyst and analysand *are* together and affect one another in the context of a neutral frame or Freudian pair. The repetition of primary narcissism, in Loewald's sense, is what Bollas calls the retrieval of enviro-somatic caregiving as "existential" memory.

Unconscious creativity is solitary *autopoiesis* or individuation, as the production of individual singularity which makes cultural production or sublimation in a traditional sense possible. In Chapter 1, in relation to Freud's thinking about primary idealizing identification, I called this *primary sublimation* as a term implied by the primitive psychical economy that Freud saw as giving rise to the superego (*qua* ego ideal), and to the sense of a future worth continuously reaching toward. Heidegger thought this primitive dimension both temporally and ontologically—as the *possibility* of psychological experience, which is not in the developmental past but in the future as what Da-sein reaches toward by radically individuating or, in psychoanalytic terms, sublimating itself. In-formative processing as temporal "printing" (Derrida's *writing*) is what is called, in that aspect of Freud's work that Bollas consistently chooses not to consider, the *economizing of the libido*, which, as Loewald argued, is *sublimation* as the *structuralization* of the psyche.

Although as I noted earlier, Bollas never uses the vocabulary of sublimation in order to describe that area of experience with which he is concerned, he certainly does not ignore the practice of artistic creativity. In fact, art is among his most frequent points of reference in describing this area of experience, which is to say that this "new form of creativity fostered only in the psychoanalytic space" is directly related to creativity in a more widely cultural sense, providing the child (and, equally, the adult) access to the cultural field at large, as possessed of the capacity to excite and to inspire. The psychoanalytic (transitional, primordially relational) frame—as the aesthetically amplified possibility of time becoming space, space becoming time—attempts to capture "the domicile of the artist who is in the unique position to create his own aesthetic moments, and find symbolic equations for psychohistorical experiences that henceforth (as text, painting) become a new reality" (Bollas 1978, pp. 390–391). Although it may appear unproductive to outside observers (who may ask, with anxious incredulity, "You go to analysis how many days a week? And you've been doing this for how long?"), analyst and analysand come to know the profound creativity of unconscious transformation that occurs in the transitional play-space (*Spielraum*) of an analytic process.

Notes

1 This was the central insight of Derrida's "Freud and the Scene of Writing" (1978), which will be further elaborated upon below and in the following chapters.

76   *Fundamental ontology of Christopher Bollas*

2 Recall Loewald's description, cited in Chapter 2, of the way in which the future is "acquired": "The id, if it can be said to represent the inherited past, the degree and quality of organization with which we are born, has a future insofar as we make it ours by acquiring it, *by imprinting on it the stamp of ego organization*. Insofar as this is an unfinished task, and to the extent to which we experience it as an unfinished, never finished task, our superego is developed" (Loewald 1988, p. 49; emphasis added).

3 For example, in *Dissemination* (1981), Derrida, sounding as if he were reading Bion and commenting on the notion of clinical reverie, writes, "To lose one's head, no longer to know where one's head is, such is perhaps the effect of dissemination" (p. 20). Bollas, in his own text titled "Dissemination" (1995) writes, "... we are all living disseminations of questioning complexities—arranged through our idioms' encounters with reality ..." (p. 55). Whatever the case may be concerning Bollas's actual familiarity with Derrida's texts, their points of convergence are at times startling, to say the least.

4 Barnaby Barratt (2013, 2016, 2019) deserves mention here for his recent trilogy of books which similarly attempt (though in the absence of any serious consideration of Bollas's thinking) to portray what should appear unexpectedly radical in the Freudian practice of free association. I have expressed my many disagreements with Barratt elsewhere (Russell 2020). Nonetheless, Barratt is one of few—and perhaps the most prominent after Bollas—analysts today who have understood that a genuinely Freudian practice is not what has been transmitted for decades under the rubric of either "classical" or "contemporary" Freudian orientations, and that a more accurately informed account of what Freud actually wrote, beyond the ways in which he is perceived through the lens of an endlessly voluminous secondary literature, would reorganize the field as having been originally in advance of what are today loudly trumpeted as disciplinary breakthroughs, but that in fact constitute a series of regressive failures truly to appreciate Freud's most revolutionary discoveries and ideas.

5 I use the term "neutrality" as synonymous with "evenly hovering attention," as Greenberg (1986) suggests is appropriate, given the relatively few actual appearances of the term neutrality in Freud's writings. This term should not be understood in anything like the formal definition provided by Anna Freud, who described analytic neutrality as taking a stand "at a point equidistant from the id, the ego, and the superego" (1936, p. 28)—a formula, it seems, for achieving an allegedly objective, "fair and balanced" position.

6 This requirement has also been emphasized by Dana Birksted-Breen who, in attempting to think time at the heart of the analytic process, and in dialogue with Bion's (1962) notion of reverie as another version of Freud's evenly suspended or free-floating attention, suggestively writes,

> This type of attention is fundamental. I call this attitude 'theory in practice' because it is more than just a technique, and rests on the whole theoretical corpus and basic structure of psychoanalysis ... Without some version of this, we have 'two people in a room' but not psychoanalysis which requires the third temporal element. The absence of this 'theory in practice' may be observed in situations of impasse. In fact I consider that impasse always has at its root the absence of that third temporal element, giving rise to concrete thinking on the part of both analyst and patient. (Birksted-Breen 2016, p. 193)

There are important clinical implications in relating Birksted-Breen, Bollas and Loewald in this manner that cannot be gone into depth here, save to say that all three thinkers would be constrained to object to the "here and now" technique associated with Betty Joseph (2013; Aguayo 2011; Blass 2011).

References

Aguayo, J. (2011). "The Role of the Patient's Remembered History and Unconscious Past in the Evolution of Betty Joseph's "Here and Now" Clinical Technique (1959–1989)." *International Journal of Psychoanalysis*, 92: 1117–1136.

Barratt, B. (2013). *What is Psychoanalysis? 100 Years after Freud's 'Secret Committee'*. New York: Routledge.

Barratt, B. (2016). *Radical Psychoanalysis: An Essay on Free Associative Praxis*. New York: Routledge.

Barratt, B. (2019). *Beyond Psychotherapy: On Becoming a (Radical) Psychoanalyst*. New York: Routledge.

Bion, W. (1962). *Learning from Experience*. London: Tavistock.

Birksted-Breen, D. (2016). "Taking Time: The Tempo of Psychoanalysis." In: *The Work of Psychoanalysis*. New York: Routledge, pp. 192–212.

Blass, R. (2011). "On the Immediacy of Unconscious Truth: Understanding Betty Joseph's "Here and Now" through Comparison with Alternative Views of It outside of and within Kleinian thinking." *International Journal of Psychoanalysis*, 92:1137–1157.

Bollas, C. (1978). "The Aesthetic Moment and the Search for Transformation." *Annual of Psychoanalysis*, 6:385–394.

Bollas, C. (1979). "The Transformational Object." *International Journal of Psycho-Analysis*, 60:97–107.

Bollas, C. (1992). *Being and Character: Psychoanalysis and Self Experience*. New York: Routledge.

Bollas, C. (1995). "Dissemination." In: *Cracking Up: The Work of Unconscious Experience*. New York: Hill and Wang.

Bollas, C. (2001). "Freudian Intersubjectivity." *Psychoanalytic Dialogues*, 11(1): 93–2015.

Bollas, C. (2002). *Free Association*. Cambridge: Icon Books.

Bollas, C. (2006). "Perceptive Identification." *Psychoanalytic Review*, 93(5):713–717

Derrida, J. (1976). *Of Grammatology*. Trans. G. Spivak. Baltimore, MD: The Johns Hopkins University Press.

Derrida, J. (1978). "Freud and the Scene of Writing." In: *Writing and Difference*. Trans. A. Bass. Chicago, IL: University of Chicago Press, pp. 196–231.

Derrida, J. (1981). *Dissemination*. Trans. B. Johnson. Chicago, IL: University of Chicago Press.

Freud, A. (1936). *The Ego and the Mechanisms of Defense*. New York: International Universities Press.

Freud, S. (1912). *Recommendations to Physicians Practising Psycho-Analysis*. S.E. XII, pp. 109–120.

Freud, S. (1919). *The "Uncanny."* S.E. XVII, pp. 217–256.

Gasché, R. (1986). *The Tain of the Mirror: Derrida and the Philosophy of Reflection*. Cambridge, MA: Harvard University Press.

Greenberg, J. (1986). "The Problem of Analytic Neutrality." *Contemporary Psychoanalysis*, 22:76–86.

Heidegger, M. (1996). *Being and Time*. Trans J. Stambaugh. New York: SUNY Press.

Joseph, B. (2013). "Here and Now: My Perspective." *International Journal of Psycho-Analysis*, 94(1):1–5.

Momigliano, L.N. (2016). "Two People Talking in a Room: An Investigation into the Analytic Dialogue." In: *Reading Italian Psychoanalysis*. Ed. F. Borgogna, A. Luchetti and L.M. Coe. New York: Routledge, pp. 347–358.

78 *Fundamental ontology of Christopher Bollas*

Nettleton, S. (2017). *The Metapsychology of Christopher Bollas*. New York: Routledge.

Reis, B. (2020). *Creative Repetition and Intersubjectivity: Contemporary Freudian Explorations of Trauma, Memory, and Clinical Process*. New York: Routledge.

Russell, J. (2019). *Psychoanalysis and Deconstruction: Freud's Psychic Apparatus*. New York: Routledge.

Russell, J. (2020). "Book Review: *What is Called Psychoanalysis?* (2013); *Radical Psychoanalysis* (2016); *and* Beyond *Psychotherapy* (2019) by Barnaby Barratt." *Psychoanalytic Psychology*, 37(2):169–172.

Winnicott, D.W. (1958). "The Capacity to be Alone." *International Journal of Psycho-Analysis*, 39:416–420.

Winnicott, D.W. (1970). *Playing and Reality*. New York: Routledge.

Winnicott, D.W. (1973). *The Child, the Family and the Outside World*. New York: Penguin Books.

4 *Antigone*—sublimation as transgressive autonomy

In *Hölderlin's Hymn "The Ister,"* Heidegger (1996b) writes,

> The Greek world is strong enough in itself to acknowledge the radiance and strength of youth and the level-headedness and wealth of experience brought by age as equally important, and to maintain the tension between them. (p. 51)

This chapter attempts a comparative reading of three major twentieth-century continental thinkers—Heidegger, Lacan and Bernard Stiegler—on the topic of Sophocles's *Antigone* as an attempt to articulate this differential tension. Although each on their own can be—and more often than not is—read as performing a critique of their predecessors, the similarities of their approaches to this most powerful of ancient Greek tragedies provides the possibility of a conceptual economy in which fundamental ontology, psychoanalysis and deconstruction mutually illuminate one another in their most radical aspects.

By examining the similarities and differences between each author's approach, I intend to demonstrate how their readings of *Antigone* reveal a complicity that demonstrates how Heideggerian fundamental ontology, Lacanian psychoanalysis, and Stiegler's materialist version of deconstruction share certain commitments that ultimately disclose the meaning of the experience of the *political* as a form of *transgression* that addresses what it means for human beings to experience *limits*. Such experiences produce a sense of what it means to be an individual, as an experience of *autonomy* as the self-giving (*autos*) of what has been inscribed historically as law (*nomos*), at both the individual and collective levels. Each author in his own way reads *Antigone* as an allegory of the process of individuation that human beings undergo as an act of *defiance* with which what is called "life" itself can be identified. For each thinker, and with respect to their readings of *Antigone,* this is the meaning of the experience of *adolescence* as an uncanny, liminal or transitional passage that links childhood to what it means to be an adult.

DOI: 10.4324/9781003243878-4

80 *Antigone*

Heidegger: *Antigone*, uncanniness, individuation

Heidegger's discussions of *Antigone* appear in the *Introduction to Metaphysics* from 1935, and in *Hölderlin's Hymn "The Ister"* from 1942. In both cases, the focus of Heidegger's attention is on the choral ode that immediately precedes the first dialogue between Antigone and Creon. In the 1942 course, Heidegger will have more to say about the specific character of Antigone and of her actions, while in the 1935 course his comments will be devoted exclusively to the second choral ode itself. Developing his earlier reflections seven years later, in the course on Hölderlin, Heidegger will famously describe Antigone as, "the supreme uncanny" (1996b, p. 104).

In the *Introduction to Metaphysics* (2000), Heidegger draws on the choral ode in order to bring to light the meaning of Parmenides's saying *to gar auto noein estin te kai einai*—customarily translated as, "thinking and being are the same." Heidegger takes this statement to be an account of human being from an "originary" Greek perspective. He attributes no small significance to what it attempts to disclose, and to the effort at seeking after this: "The saying became the guiding principle of Western philosophy only after it was no longer understood, because its originary truth could not be held fast. The Greeks themselves began to fall away from the truth of the saying right after Parmenides" (p. 154).

Greek tragedy, according to Heidegger, will be crucial in grasping the meaning of the statement of Parmenides because tragedy is the "proper counterpart" to the "poetizing thinking" that characterizes pre-Socratic philosophy. It is in tragedy that, "Greek Being and Da-sein were authentically founded" (p. 154). The choral ode to which Heidegger devotes his attention is particularly relevant here in that it constitutes "a poetic projection of Being-human among the Greeks" (p. 156).

Heidegger's approach focuses largely on unpacking the first two lines by continuously returning to them while reading the rest of the passage as an elaboration of the central insight they contain:

> Manifold is the uncanny, yet nothing
>
> uncannier than man bestirs itself, rising up beyond him. (p. 156)

Heidegger will be at pains to demonstrate that naming the human being as the uncanniest—*to deinotaton*—does not indicate a quality of the human being, even an essential quality. The uncanniness of the human being is not a quality that can be appreciated by an attitude capable only of grasping what is "present-at-hand" (objectively present), as one quality among many or as a position that the human being might take up after having been determined in advance as human. Uncanniness here is intended to indicate something about the world itself in which the human being participates to a fundamental extent, and in a way that shapes both. The "manifold" describes the world itself,

Antigone 81

in relation to which the human is the uncanniest of the uncanny in that it participates in this world in a particular and eventful (historical) way.

In *Being and Time* (1996a) Heidegger had distinguished the everyday sense of the uncanny, in which the familiar is suddenly and momentarily experienced as unfamiliar, from "primordial uncanniness." The latter functions as a lever to open up an analysis of Da-sein as always already ahead of itself or as outside itself as in-the-world. The former manifests the effort of the they-self (*das Man*) to flee primordial uncanniness, in which Da-sein is inherently not at home in the world. Da-sein's not-being-at-home in the world is primordial because Da-sein is not at home with itself but always ahead of or outside of itself, which is another of way of stating that it *is as* being-in-the-world.

In the *Introduction to Metaphysics*, Heidegger's analysis of the second choral ode begins by calling into question the translation of the Greek *deinon* into the ordinary German term *unheimlich* because the translation itself performs the same fleeing function of the they-self from the real experience of what is at issue: "The *deinon* is the terrible sense of the overwhelming sway, which induces panicked fear, true anxiety, as well as collected, inwardly reverberating, reticent awe. The violent, the overwhelming is the essential character of the sway itself" (p. 159). Later in the text, Heidegger will identify this "sway" with the Greek word *phusis*, typically translated as nature. What he is describing here is the world as manifold not merely in the sense of the complex but in the sense of the threatening, and threatening in a primordial way: "When the sway breaks in, it *can* keep its overwhelming power to itself. But this does not make it more harmless but only *more* terrible and distant" (p. 160; emphases in original).

The violence of that which is primordially *deinon* is equally demonstrated by the uncanniest of the uncanny (the human), about which Heidegger says, "using violence is the basic trait not just of his doing but of his Da-sein" (p. 160). Heidegger is quick to distinguish this violence from violence in the ordinary sense of disturbance and offense. At stake is a kind of primordial violence that will deepen the analysis of the primordial uncanniness of the human being—again, its being-outside-itself as always already in-the-world. The basic trait of this violence-doing consists in the mode of Da-sein's going forth in relation to an experience of limits: "as those who do violence, they overstep the limits of the homely, precisely in the direction of the uncanny in the sense of of the overwhelming" (p. 161). Heidegger reads this as reflected in the choral verse, "Everywhere trying out, underway; untried, with no way out he comes to nothing," which he interprets to mean that human beings make routes (*poros*) within the world as overwhelming sway, in the form of a going over to, which exposes them to disaster:

> *as* violence-doing they drive themselves beyond what is homely for them, but in all this they first become the uncanniest, because now, as those who on all ways have no way out, they are thrown out of all relation to the homely, and *atē*, ruin, calamity overtakes them. (p. 162; emphasis in original)

82   *Antigone*

Heidegger then draws attention to the appearance of the word *polis* in the text and its structural similarity to the way in which routes or paths (*poros*) appear. The *polis* is, according to Heidegger, to be interpreted as the place in which all routes cross. This place is essentially constituted not as a *state* but as a *site*: "the Here, within which and as which Being-here is historically. The *polis* is the site of history, the Here, *in* which, *out of* which and *for* which history happens" (p. 162; emphases in original). In this way, poets appear *as* poets, thinkers appear *as* thinkers and rulers appear *as* rulers. It is this as-structure in which the constitutive violence of Da-sein consists. Rising in history from the site of the *polis*, as the place or Here at which all paths cross, human beings are exposed to ruin, becoming uncanny—without place or home—as again always already outside or ahead of themselves.

In turning his attention to the ode beyond its initial appeal to the human as the uncanniest of the uncanny, Heidegger interprets the chorus's account of the subjugation of nature by human beings. But the violence of which he speaks is not reducible to any act of subjugation. The subjugation of sea and earth and animal of which the ode speaks does not consist in the reduction of these manifestations of the manifold uncanny or "sway" to instruments serving human purposes. What is primordially violent in this act of subjugation is that these phenomena are first opened up in their being and first begin to appear *as* themselves: "This breaking forth, this breaking up, capturing and subjugating is in itself the first opening of beings *as* sea, *as* earth, *as* animal" (p. 167; emphases in original). This uncanny violence (*deinon*) belongs, according to Heidegger, first and foremost to language, as that which appears nearest to human being but is "still more distant and more overwhelming than sea and earth." For Heidegger, this is because the power of poetizing is its capacity to render something as that which it is.

Heidegger is here further developing—as he will do for the rest of his life—his analysis of what, in paragraph 32 of *Being and Time,* and as we saw in Chapter 2, he had called the "as-structure of being." This is a structure underlying the possibility of understanding that lies before both meaning and objectivity. In paragraph 69 of *Being and Time*, he will demonstrate the as-structure to be grounded in the structure of Da-sein as ecstatic temporality: being-toward as being-in-a-world as being-together-with. Encountering something *as* something (sea *as* sea, earth *as* earth, etc.) is an act of interpretation by means of which Da-sein's being-in-the-world is always already disclosed, if forgotten, and as such it is primarily concerned with "the explicitness of something that is understood":

> The "as" constitutes the structure of the explicitness of what is understood; it constitutes the interpretation [*Ausgelegte*]. The circumspect, interpretive association with what is at hand in the surrounding world which "sees" this *as* a table, a door, a car, a bridge does not necessarily already have to analyze [*auseinander zu legen*] what is circumspectly interpreted in a particular *statement*. Any simple prepredicative seeing

Antigone   83

of what is at hand is in itself already understanding and interpretative. (1996a, p. 140; emphases in original)

The as-structure is thus a pre-predicative differential tension that both connects and separates, making possible experiences of both subjective meaning and objective fact. Passively seeing something *as* something is itself a structure of interpretation that is not performed by Da-sein, but is that which Da-sein always already is in its being-outside-itself—its uncanniness. The human being is the uncanniest of the uncanny because it is historical; history is made possible by the *historicity* that the *Introduction to Metaphysics* thinks as primordial violence:

> The violence-doing of poetic saying, or thoughtful projection, of constructive building, of state creating action, is not an application of faculties that the human being has, but is a disciplining and disposing of the violent forces by virtue of which beings disclose themselves as such, insofar as the human being enters into them. This disclosedness of beings is the violence that humanity has to surmount in order to be itself first of all—that is, to be historical in doing violence in the midst of beings. (2000, p. 167)

This "disciplining" is again not an ordinary act of subjugation; it concerns rather precisely that of which the chorus speaks as that which absolutely cannot be subjugated:

> A single onslaught, death, he was unable
> ever to resist by any flight,
> even if in the face of dire illness
> deft escape should be granted him. (p. 157)

Death, says Heidegger, is "an end beyond all completion, a limit beyond all limits" (p. 168). As such it is not, as the analysis of being-toward-death in Division Two of *Being and Time* had made clear, a merely anticipated future possibility:

> The human being has no way out in the face of death, not only when it is time to die, but constantly and essentially. Insofar as human beings *are*, they stand in the no-exit of death. Thus Being-here is the happening of un-canniness itself. (p. 169; emphasis in original)

Death as the "limit beyond all limits" is the articulated separation-connection of the human being's uncanniness, violence-doing and being ahead or outside-itself as always already being-in-a-world. What *Being and Time* had called the as-structure of being is the violence-doing that is the "basic trait" of Da-sein because in making beings appear as beings, paths (*poros*) cross at, or rather *as*

84 *Antigone*

the site (*polis*) of history. Thus, according to Heidegger, "With the naming of *this* violent and uncanny thing [death], the poetic projection of Being and of the human essence sets its own limits for itself" (ibid.; emphasis in original)

This setting of limits is the "disciplining and disposing of the violent forces by virtue of which beings disclose themselves as such, insofar as the human being enters into them." Heidegger will describe this setting of limits in terms of the appearance of two phenomena central to the Greek understanding of human being: *technē* (knowing) and *dikē* (justice).

In the first instance—*technē* as knowing—Heidegger is quick to distinguish the Greek sense of this term from the modern technological sense as the gathering of information about what is present-at-hand. Knowing, rather, is "the ability to set Being into work as something this in each case *is* in such and such a way" (p. 170; emphasis in original). The privileged example of *technē* for Heidegger, here as elsewhere, is art. A work of art is not a work because materials are worked upon, but because art discloses or "puts to work" being in beings. To put to work being in beings is to make things stand forth as they are. This is the sense in which *technē* is an opening-up and a keeping-open that is essentially, primordially violent. For Heidegger here, the violence of knowing is the violence of passion, and, "*The passion of knowing is questioning*" (p. 170; emphasis added). This is what makes *technē* a manifestation of that which is *deinon* (violent, uncanny).

In the second instance—*dikē* as justice—Heidegger is again quick to remind us that the Greek sense of the term is not primarily juridical or moral in its reference. Nor does it primarily indicate an orientation toward normativity. *Dikē* indicates rather more originally arrangement or "fittingness" (*Fug*), in the sense of jointedness, articulation and structure.[1] This, he says, describes, "the direction that the overwhelming gives to its sway" and "the enjoining structure, which compels fitting-in and compliance" (p. 171). This is the violence of justice, in the properly Greek sense, and it is why justice, like knowing, is also a manifestation of that which is *deinon*. The proper domain of justice is not the *polis* in the ordinary sense of the sphere of the political, but *phusis,* and not in the everyday sense of the natural but as that which is most moving and overwhelming.

Finally then, Heidegger posits justice (*dikē*) as the overwhelming, and knowing (*technē*) as violence-doing. Both are manifestations of what is most primordially violent, uncanny (*deinon*). Recall that Heidegger's analysis had begun by ascribing this essential characteristic to both the human being and the world, as a way of thinking human being as in-the-world, prior to any form of external opposition between them as between things when they appear merely present-at-hand or in objective presence. This is the meaning of death as the "limit beyond all limits" that establishes Da-sein as an instance of the as-structure according to which beings may appear *as* beings. Heidegger has given here perhaps his most forceful articulation of how Da-sein, as in-the-world, and as always already outside-itself, is not *of* the world but *unheimlich*, that is: *always already dead*. This is what it means for human beings to be

Antigone　85

historical beings, as the relation of knowing and justice: "*Dikē* is the over-whelming fittingness. *Technē* is the violence-doing of knowing. The reciprocal relation between them is the happening of uncanniness" (p. 176).

The reciprocity of this relation, on Heidegger's account, is what allows the human being to be a historical being—it is a relational reciprocity that *his-toricizes*. The being that pursues the overwhelming fittingness of that which is through the pursuit of knowing as the passion for questioning is not one who historicizes in order to bring about community, law and knowledge in their ordinary, politico-juridical sense. To the contrary, he or she is one who breaks open anything resembling community, law or knowledge in an act of violence that makes of the one who does so a creator in the most radical sense of the word: *breaking* with tradition by *grounding* tradition anew. This is why Heidegger sees in Greek tragedy the "proper counterpart" to the "poetizing thinking" that characterizes pre-Socratic philosophy and in particular the saying of Parmenides that "thinking and being are the same." It is the violence of this saying that Greek tragedy—and *Antigone* in particular—most clearly illuminates, for Heidegger. This is because, where the saying of Parmenides is concerned, "it is a matter of the inceptive, poetizing-thinking, grounding and founding of the historical Da-sein of a people" (p. 176). As Heidegger portrays it, tragedy stages this grounding as a form of poetizing, by disclosing a *disaster* beyond recognition:

> Therefore the violence-doer knows no kindness and conciliation (in the ordinary sense), no appeasement and mollification by success and prestige and by their confirmation. In all this, the violence-doer as creator sees only a seeming fulfillment, which is to be despised. In willing the unprecedented, the violence-doer casts aside all help. For such a one, disaster is the deepest and broadest Yes to the overwhelming. (p. 174)

It becomes clear at this end point in his analysis that, although she is never named, it is the character of Antigone herself that Heidegger has in mind, and that it is Antigone herself he has been discussing all along as she informs his interpretation of the choral ode. Antigone, who upon her sentence is praised by the chorus, and who rebukes this as mere consolation, who insistently refuses mollification and prestige with all her being, violently casts aside care in an ordinary sense no matter how much it is offered to her, and yet who manifests a "primordial" attitude of care (*Sorge*) in her defiance and in her commitment to her brother, which has nothing to do with the law of the family as traditional interpretations of the play would have it. This is what Heidegger had designated as the uncanniest of the uncanny—Antigone is the uncanniest of the uncanniest of the uncanny—in that she relentlessly pursues disaster, and as a way of affirming the overwhelming that will be left out in the open, interpreted as disclosed, like the body of her brother and uncle Polynices, for those who (like Creon) will as a result live on as exposed in their being already dead in the wake of her creative, grounding action. Antigone has

86 *Antigone*

the passion for questioning authority, and for *pursuing justice* as that which is *most overwhelmingly violent*. Antigone's acts of *defiance* are acts of *interpretation* in an existential or ontologically primordial sense, in which the violence of the as-structure of being appears most nakedly and overwhelmingly as it *is*. This is what is most overwhelming in this most overwhelming of Greek tragedies.

In reference to the last lines of the second choral ode ("Let him not become a companion at my hearth/not let my knowing see such delusions/of the one who works such deeds"), Heidegger writes,

> One who *is* in *this way* (namely, as the uncanniest) should be excluded from hearth and counsel. Nevertheless, the chorus's concluding words do not contradict what it previously says about Being-human. Insofar as the chorus turns *against* the uncanniest, it says that this manner of Being is *not* the everyday one. (p. 175; emphases in original)

In *Hölderlin's Hymn "The Ister"* (1996b), Heidegger makes clear that the "harmless" (p. 93) interpretation that mistakes Creon for the uncanny one who is to be cast out of the chorus's hearth, regarding Antigone as the one who remains inside, purified of that which is *deinon*, fails to appreciate what is at actually stake in the text. Heidegger's Antigone is the one who is most outside the everyday, whose Da-sein is most outside or ahead of itself as violently in-the-world, and in such a way as to be indicative of this violence that is the "basic trait" of the human being as the uncanniest of the uncanny that is the manifold. This is why she is properly a creator in the "Greek" sense, in that she leaves her world absolutely and irretrievably transformed.

Lacan: *Antigone*, desire, sublimation

Lacan's reading of *Antigone* in his 1959–1960 seminar *The Ethics of Psychoanalysis* is for the most part so recognizably similar to Heidegger's own reading as to appear almost derivative. Translating Heidegger's "over-whelming sway" (*phusis*) into his own theoretical register as the Real or the Thing, Lacan seems in retrospect to have little that is new to add to Heidegger's account of what previous commentators had missed in their approach to Antigone as the embodiment of the proto-Platonic Good. But in attempting to cast this reading in psychoanalytic terms, Lacan in fact adds a crucial dimension to our understanding of what Heidegger had meant by a being constitutively in excess of all limits yet driven in its being always already outside itself to discipline the forces of violence-doing in the reciprocal relationship of *technē* and *dikē* or of Da-sein and world.

Like Heidegger, Lacan finds in *Antigone* "the essence of tragedy" (1992, p. 247). And again like Heidegger, Lacan places the question of death and the question of the experience of limits at the center of his analysis of the text and of Greek tragedy in general. Antigone is treated as one "who find[s] themselves right away in a limit zone, find themselves between life and death"

Antigone 87

(p. 272). He characterizes Antigone in this way even before she is shut up in the tomb as punishment for her crimes by Creon, seeing in this event a dramatization of the place in which she has been from the beginning of the play: "she crosses the entrance to the zone between life and death, that is to say, when what she has already affirmed herself to be takes on an outward form" (p. 280). At one point adopting an explicitly Heideggerian vocabulary to articulate this between-zone (there are references to Heidegger in the text, but never to the *Introduction to Metaphysics*), he states,

> This is the point where the false metaphors of being (*l'etant*) can be distinguished from the position of Being (*l'etre*) itself, and we find its place articulated as such, as a limit, throughout the text of *Antigone*, in the mouths of all the characters and of Tiresias. (p. 248)

It is the effort to outline this limit that Lacan will claim is the central preoccupation of his seminar on *The Ethics of Psychoanalysis*.

Lacan is quick to distance himself from Hegel's reading of *Antigone*, which represents the standard according to which Antigone and Creon are to be seen as opposed to one another, with Creon representing the laws of the city and Antigone representing the laws of the family and of the Gods (*dikē*). This reductive approach will link Hegel to the "bidet-water commentary that is typical of the style used by those virtuous writers who write about her" (p. 262)—an approach that Heidegger had similarly dismissed as "harmless" and uninformed. At stake in the text, for Lacan, is rather the relation of the subject to the limit, and of course in the end this will have to do, for Lacan, and once again like Heidegger, with the relation to language.

"The limit involved," says Lacan,

> the limit that it is essential to situate if a certain phenomenon is to emerge through reflection, is something I have called the phenomenon of the beautiful, it is something I have begun to define as the limit of the second death. (p. 260)

By "second death" Lacan references a death that occurs even after, if not before, death in an ordinary sense has transpired. He reads, for example, Hamlet's inability to kill Claudius while he is praying not as a form of neurotic hesitation but as a refusal to allow for the possibility that Claudius might go to heaven if he is killed during such a pious act; Hamlet does not want merely to kill Claudius but to ensure that in addition to being killed his soul will go to hell. It is not enough that someone might be removed from life but that they die in a way that maximizes their death and suffering. Lacan claims that he had made this distinction and outlined the liminal zone between life and death first in relation to Sade's texts, where, "suffering doesn't lead the victim to the point where he is dismembered and destroyed. It seems rather that the object of all the torture is to retain the capacity of being an indestructible support"

88 *Antigone*

(p. 261). The result is the disclosure of a dimension Lacan calls the "play of pain," which links Sade's texts to the proper discourse of aesthetics. The victims in Sade's texts always appear as beautiful and adorned, and it is this aspect that is constantly under attack, not the subjectivity of the victim. This, for Lacan, draws a striking parallel with Kant's analysis of beauty in the *Critique of Judgment*, in which the object itself is not involved:

> I take it you see the analogy with the Sadean fantasm, since the object there is no more than the power to support a form of suffering, which is in itself nothing else than the signifier of a limit. Suffering is conceived as a stasis which affirms that that which is cannot return to the void from which it emerged. (ibid.)

Like Heidegger, Lacan conceives the limit Antigone intends to cross in terms of *atē*—ruin: "It is an irreplaceable word. It designates the limit that human life can only briefly cross ... Beyond this *Atē,* one can only spend a brief period of time, and that's where Antigone wants to go" (pp. 262–263). For Heidegger, it is this insistence that makes Antigone "the supreme uncanny." For Lacan, it is what takes her "beyond the limits of the human," in that her desire takes her into "the beyond of *Atē*" as this liminal zone between life and death or "between two deaths," and toward the second death which can be read as a form of uncanny, differential (individuating) repetition.

Lacan even offers his own extensive analysis of the choral ode which had so preoccupied Heidegger, as "a celebration of mankind" (p. 274). In approaching the choral ode in the way that he does, Lacan is closer than Heidegger to those "bidet-water commentaries" that he otherwise works to avoid, translating the opening lines as, "There are a lot of wonders in the world, but there is nothing more wonderful than man" (ibid.). But his reading demonstrates a rigor that draws on an explicitly clinical, psychoanalytic register.

With reference to Levi-Strauss, Lacan sees in the "wonder" (*deinon*) of man of which the chorus speaks the distinction between culture and nature: "man cultivates speech and the sublime sciences; he knows how to protect his dwelling place from winter frosts and from the blasts of a storm; he knows how to avoid getting wet" (ibid.). It is, at the outset at least, a question of knowledge that the chorus speaks of, for Lacan. Lacan sees nothing of the violence that Heidegger had portrayed in all this, or of knowing as a form of violence-doing. And yet in his own way he does see this violence-doing as a basic trait of the human being, regarding this as an irreducible violence that the human being does *to itself.*

Lacan interprets the chorus's praise for the "resourcefulness" of man not as a statement concerning the power of the human being, but rather as a statement that "man knows a lot of tricks," linking this to the notion of *aporia* (from *a-poros*—without a path), which he takes to be an indication that the human being is the one who is "screwed" (p. 275). It is not the case, for Lacan, that

Antigone 89

the resourcefulness of the human being makes it capable of dealing with any situation with which nature confronts it, as most commentators would discover in this passage from the choral ode. Rather, the resourcefulness of the human means that when faced with a situation in which it finds itself "screwed," the human being has the infinite capacity *to make things worse for itself*. When backed into a corner by circumstance, says Lacan, the human being is possessed of a "wonderful" capacity to respond by ruining itself. This is why he casts *atē* in the form of a limit that is crossed: "He [man] knows what he's doing. He always manages to cause things to come crashing down on his head" (ibid.).

At the point at which the chorus invokes death as that which the human being ultimately cannot ever escape, which for Heidegger represents a horizon of possibility that projects Da-sein outside or ahead of itself, Lacan makes a highly idiosyncratic charge against the standard translation of the lines that follow. This is the specific site where Lacan's psychoanalytic perspective begins to open up, and that will guide his further reading. Heidegger modifies the opening lines of the verse, but unlike Lacan he does not tend to the later lines. The translation Heidegger (2000) provides is:

> Everywhere trying out, underway; untried, with no way out
> he comes to Nothing.
> A single onslaught, death, he was unable
> ever to resist by any flight,
> even in the face of dire illness
> deft escape should be granted him. (p. 157)

Heidegger's move, as we saw, was to demonstrate a paradox in the verse's opening lines that contraindicates the standard translation and reading of the passage as suggesting that the resourcefulness of the human being is infinite, even though death marks a certain impenetrable limit. Like Lacan, Heidegger sees that the passage indicates rather the irreducibility of *atē* given the constitutive relationship between Da-sein and death as its own-most (*Eigentlich*) radical possibility.

What Lacan does is to call into question on this basis the reading of the last lines of the verse concerning the relationship between the human being and illness. Against the standard reading of the last two lines, according to which human beings remain resourceful with respect to overcoming illness, on Lacan's reading of the original Greek, the human being, who "knows all kinds of tricks," is capable of escaping not *from* but *into* "impossible sicknesses":

> The translations usually attempt to say that man even manages to come to deal with sickness, but that's not what it means at all. He hasn't managed to come to terms with death but he invents marvelous gimmicks in the form of sicknesses he fabricates himself. (Lacan 1992, p. 275)

90   *Antigone*

What Lacan appears to be getting at here should remind us of what Heidegger had said when he wrote, "With the naming of this violent and uncanny thing, the poetic projection of Being and of the human essence sets its own limits for itself" (2000, p. 169). For Lacan, the foundational establishment of a limit is the "signifying cut" that relates the subject to language and that makes of the subject an "indestructible support" which "cannot return to the void from which it emerged." It is from this that issues Antigone's defiance of the order of Creon, in which she is able to affirm the signifier of the blood relation "brother" in the Real and to distinguish this from every other form of relationship which she might take up as arbitrary and replaceable (husband, child, etc.). "When she explains to Creon what she has done," says Lacan, "Antigone affirms the advent of the absolute individual with the phrase, 'That's how it is because that's how it is'" (p. 278).

For Heidegger, too, this disclosure of Da-sein's primordial uncanniness or violence is an act of individuation—of "the most radical individuation" (Heidegger 1996a, p. 34)—that is at once a radical and constitutive setting of limits, limits which are also always already crossed. For Lacan, "Involved is an horizon determined by a structural relation; it only exists on the basis of the language of words, but it reveals their unsurpassable consequence" (Lacan 1992, p. 278). Antigone thus appears for Lacan as,

> a pure simple relationship of the human being to that of which he miraculously happens to be the bearer, namely, the signifying cut that confers on him the indomitable power of being what he is in the face of everything that may oppose him. (p. 282)

We should be careful, however, not to reduce Lacan's reading of the play to a second rate imitation of Heidegger, because while there are clearly strong and obvious parallels, Lacan introduces into the horizon of Heideggerian reflection an element that Heidegger himself fails to elaborate upon—and this is *not* the addition of a concern for the place of language for the human being, of which Heidegger was perfectly well aware, and about which he had already said much the same thing as Lacan, in the absence of the jargon of linguistics and of the "signifying cut."[2]

Where Lacan makes his most original mark lies in his treatment of the aesthetic dimension of the play and the question as to the relationship between Antigone and the beautiful. There is no mention of beauty in Heidegger's treatment of the overwhelming sway, or of the reciprocal relationship between *technē* and *dikē*. Referencing Kant's *Critique of Judgment*, Lacan asks how it is that Antigone can appear to us today—as products of a Christian heritage to which the Greek audience had not been subjected—as a figure of such sublime and terrifying beauty. It is this fact, says Lacan, that repeatedly leaves traditional commentators foundering when they situate Antigone outside the realm of *atē* and see in her a figure of the sublime good or the purity of the martyr. Lacan emphasizes the date of the play's production (441BC) to the extent that it not only antedates by centuries the advent of Christianity, but comes even a century before Plato's identification of the beautiful with the Good (p. 259, 285; on this point, see also Themi 2014, pp. 41–63). This is why *Antigone* holds such a privileged place in the history of tragedy and its reception in the Christian world, and why it is in *Antigone* that both Heidegger and Lacan will locate the essence of tragedy:

> We know very well that over and beyond the dialogue, over and beyond the question of family and country, over and beyond the moralizing arguments, it is Antigone herself who fascinates us, Antigone in her unbearable splendor. She has a quality that both attracts us and startles us, in the sense of intimidates us, this terrible, self-willed victim disturbs us. (Lacan 1992, p. 247)

It would seem to be this very question of a disturbing, "unbearable splendor" that motivates Lacan even to include a series of lectures on *Antigone* in the context of his seminar on ethics understood from a psychoanalytic perspective. What might on the surface appear to be a supplementary excursus on a particular literary text in fact articulates what Lacan is after throughout the seminar in the form of an account of the relationship between the subject and what he calls *das Ding* (the Heideggerian resonance of the term is inescapably obvious). It is here that Lacan will inaugurate what will become a major shift in his later teachings from desire to the drive, and from a concern with the Symbolic and the Imaginary to the Real. At stake is the question of an other side to the Kantian thematic of the sublime in the form of that which is monstrous, such that the object of desire is at once both attractive and repulsive, compelling to the point of crossing of a limit that "unknowingly" invites us to ruin (*atē*). But it is also at this point that Lacan tends toward abandoning his early, Hegelian commitment to the question of desire, and begins to focus instead on what he thinks as the circular movement of the drive (*Trieb*).

In approaching the text in just this way, Lacan's commentary on *Antigone* extends his commentary earlier in the seminar on the topic of sublimation. Antigone appears in her unbearable splendor to the extent that she is capable of demonstrating this act in its purest and most basic sense. It is between Antigone and the decomposing body of her brother Polynices that Lacan situates the capacity of sublimation to raise the object to the dignity of the Thing (p. 112). It is not Antigone herself who accomplishes this task; but in doubling herself (p. 261), like Sade's Justine, for example, to stand out as an indestructible support for whatever punishments she might incur, Antigone stands *against* a social value system that would continue to think naively in terms of the simple tension between the family and the state—a tension that Plato would attempt to reconcile in the project of the *Republic*, missing or covering over entirely what Lacan draws our attention to when he orients

92   *Antigone*

our understanding toward a good that "cannot reign over all without an excess emerging whose fatal consequences are revealed to us in tragedy" (p. 259). This is the good of Creon, who everywhere demonstrates this ideal good of the community to be shot through by his own drive for authority and power. This is the Good of Plato for which Lacan seeks a before, a gesture of taking desire to a limit that is precisely not defined in established or normative social or cultural terms.

Of sublimation, Lacan had earlier in the seminar stated,

> It is a paradoxical fact that the drive is able to find its aim elsewhere than in that which is its aim—without its being a question of the signifying substitution that constitutes the overdetermined structure, the ambiguity, and the double causality, of the symptom as compromise formation. (p. 110)

Lacan's unique approach to the concept allows him to sidestep the endemic difficulties he notes all other authors encounter in attempting to do the same.[3] These difficulties have to do with failure to understand the relationship between sublimation and repression, which is itself a result of the field's failure to understand the absolute difference between the biological *Instinkt* and the properly Freudian notion of *Trieb*:

> The sublimation that provides the *Trieb* with a satisfaction different from its aim—an aim that is still defined as its natural aim—is precisely that which reveals the true nature of the *Trieb* insofar as it is not simply instinct, but has a relationship to *das Ding* as such, to the Thing insofar as it is distinct from the object. (p. 111)

It is the act of sublimation itself as a vicissitude of the drive with respect to its aim, Lacan indicates, that creates the Thing in distinguishing it from the object as something both terrifying and sublime.

We must not miss why Lacan situates this activity with regard to the question of *ethics*, which is at once a *social* question no matter how much Lacan otherwise wishes to dissimulate this fact: "It is after all as a function of of the problem of ethics that we have to judge sublimation; it creates socially recognized values" (p. 107). It is for this reason, as Heidegger had already indicated, that Antigone is properly a creator, one who creates social values by means of an act of radical defiance. Antigone sublimates herself, individuating herself by distinguishing herself from being the object of Creon's rule, raising herself up to the dignity of the Thing and thereby demonstrating an unbearable splendor that is still to this day recognizable. In Lacanian terms, this is her status "between two deaths," as the crossing of a limit that reveals her being as substantial support no matter what punishment she suffers. Unlike her docile and complacent sister Ismene, Antigone affirms that her fate has already been destined to be tragic because her family is one in which she appears in her being *as* the crossing of an absolute limit, her father being also her brother.

What *Antigone* thus demonstrates for Lacan is that sublimation is the paradigmatic case of the "impossible sicknesses" that the human being is capable of escaping again not *from* but *into* in the face of the inescapable limit of death. By introducing the psychoanalytic question of the sublimation of the drive into the ontological framework that Heidegger had provided, Lacan's central contribution is the key insight—one that distinguishes Lacan's from all other analytic approaches to the topic, and in a way that radicalizes what Heidegger had thought as the essential violence-doing of Da-sein in its being always already outside itself—that true sublimation, which is not just about cultural production, but about the creation of new "socially recognized values," is always and irreducibly an act of *transgression*.

Stiegler: *Antigone,* generation, defiance

Stiegler approaches *Antigone* from his own uniquely materialist version of deconstruction, one that is in excess of Derrida's attachment to the literary object, and that bears no relation to the vapid proliferation of "deconstructionism" among those who seek only to imitate Derrida's intermittently high modern textual style. Stiegler reads in *Antigone* a way of thinking the politics of the intergenerational transmission of knowledge in the form of idealities that constitute the horizon of a sustainable future. It is the threat to this sustainability around which his later work on the era of the Anthropocene came to be organized, and in one of his last works he invoked Antigone in order to pay homage to the environmental activist Greta Thunberg (Stiegler 2020).

In *Uncontrollable Societies of Disaffected Individuals* (2013), Stiegler provides his most sustained engagement with an analysis of *Antigone,* and with what the play has to offer in terms of our ability to cultivate a contemporary perspective on the diminishing returns of a civilization in which the dynamic evolution of technology has overtaken the capacity of the human to maintain its own equilibrium. Most generally and across his interventions, Stiegler elaborated on Derrida's understanding of the role that technical, material inscription has historically played in the evolution of human beings' capacity to form elaborate systems of memorization that make possible the emergence of what Stiegler calls *consistencies,* which in themselves do not formally *exist* but which *persist* in their capacity to orient human beings toward a future worth not only cultivating but fighting for. In, "The Antigone Complex," Stiegler identifies *dikē* (justice) and *aidos* (shame) as values that emerged from out of the Greek cultivation of systems of symbolic, materialist articulations (writing) that would open up the possibility of passing these ideals down to future generations, far beyond any regional or historical context.

Like Lacan, Stiegler recognizes that what psychoanalysis offers in the form of a theory of sublimation is a theory of transgression as formative of socially

94   *Antigone*

recognized and therefore historically transmissible values. This is a further articulation of what Heidegger had meant by the fundamental violence-doing of the being that is irreducibly outside-itself as primordially uncanny (*deinon*). Unlike Lacan, whose clinical focus led him to emphasize an ethics of the individual not giving up on his or her desire, Stiegler's concern is rather with a thinking about sublimation as transgression in the form of a critique or judgment (*krinein*) concerning the place of the unexpected in any effort on the part of the old to produce in the young a horizon of future expectation: "*Politics… at least in its initial idea, is the organization of a sublime form of transgression*—which is also an original process of psychic, social, and technical individuation" (2013, p. 31; emphasis in original).

For Stiegler, *Antigone* primarily concerns the politically constituted orientation of a gerontocracy in its rule over the young in its effort to confer *citizenship*, which is to say a sense of *responsibility* that is at once both personal and collective. *Antigone* is, in other words, for Stiegler, at bottom an allegory about the relationship between the old and the young, and thus a staging of the dynamic relationship between control and defiance that has driven the course of Western civilization, but that is witnessing its breakdown in our current hyper-technological *qua* hyper-modern—and *not* "post-modern"— environment. Where the technological gives way to the era of digitalization, overtaking the ever-accelerating dynamics of industrialization and the advent of industrialized labor (the consequences of which Freud, by 1930, was already well aware), what we are witnessing is the breakdown of any capacity for generational transfer or *transference*, which is to say of any historically recognizable form of what it means for children to live from out of and through a love for their parents:

> The acceleration of technological innovation puts young people in the difficult position of having to *initiate their parents into the reality principle,* which is constantly being transformed according to the functional conditions of new apparatus. They therefore find themselves having to initiate them into those questions through which society is trying, if possible, inasmuch as it is possible, to invent itself, and this is, perhaps for this very reason—owing to the this *reversal* of the order of generations—very difficult, if not impossible. (p. 41; emphases in original)

This reversal of the roles between the generations is at once an entropic pull toward a degradation of the relations between the generations that is now overseen by technical evolution itself. Digitalization is the accelerated generalization of this tendency, generating in the young a sense that their parents are *hopeless* in their ability to come to terms with contemporary technical demands. The normal adolescent sentiment that one is not understood by one's parents, that adults do not or cannot see the world as one does, has increasingly come to reflect an environmentally determined *fact* as children become more and more competent than their parents at navigating a technologically saturated environment, the evolutionary dynamic of which becomes more and more difficult for older generations (and thus, soon, younger generations) to keep up with. There can be a tremendous satisfaction or jouissance in this recognition, one that further reinforces how the future is nothing to be inherited from the old and is instead to be invented solely by the idealism of the young, without being informed by tradition, which can as a result *only* appear as constraint and prejudice. This sentiment is what makes the young increasingly more vulnerable to manipulation by market forces without their being able critically to recognize where this is the case or what its effects look like.

For Stiegler, *Antigone* dramatizes already the intrinsic threat of this reversal in the relationship between the old and the young, in the context of which the sublimation of the aim of the drive as the constitution of desire is overtaken by a regression from desire to a generalized reign of the drives as infinitely manipulable by the demands of the marketplace. Creon appears as the anticipation of the rule of global market relations in the place of genuine authority, in that he fails miserably to embody what traditional interpreters of the play regard as the "law of the state" or political community, with which the laws of the gods or family are thought to be in a relation of opposition, rather than in what Stiegler calls a relation of *composition*. What appears on the surface to be a relation of opposition is in reality a form of irreducible relationality or what Stiegler, following Simondon, calls transduction, as an instance of what Derrida called *différance*, in which no term appears or can sustain itself in the absence of the other.

Antigone therefore appears, on Stiegler's reading, as an account of what happens when the traditional relationship between the generations is reversed, such that it is the young who have to teach the old about what justice (*dikē*), shame (*aidos*) and authority (as the *différance* of the generations) truly mean and provide access to. This reversal is nothing new, in the sense that its dynamic has never before been present. Quite the contrary, as *Antigone* demonstrates, this reversal is the essence of the pursuit of justice in the form of the defiance of the young against the old, of the *spirit* or *desire* of those who find themselves in the *process* of formation as responsible citizens are charged with. Antigone embodies this process; Creon represents its closure in the form of an established knowledge of what is good for all in the form of a community, which Plato would subordinate under the sign of an eternal and universal Good.

Lacan had oriented his critique of this Good around the question of the disjunction between the individual and the community, seeing in this disjunction the emergence of an individual desire that could be revealed clinically, in relation to the singularity of each individual subject in their constitutive relationship to jouissance. Stiegler intrinsically makes the more formal claim that this clinical insight in fact *already* informed the constitution of Greek citizenship as the constitution of the political in a relationship of *responsibility* that binds one generation to the next in the form of a tradition, as

96 *Antigone*

a crucial aspect of what Heidegger had called *historicity*, and that makes of the young those who *sublimate* so as to *constitute* what Freud had called the superego, as something that is not simply handed down but must constantly be cultivated, reinvented and created anew. Like the Lacanian Thing, Stiegler sees that the Freudian superego does not preexist its status as sublime and therefore authoritative outside a relationship between the generations that is organized according to a certain dynamic of transference—a dynamic that is everywhere being disrupted today by the contemporary marketplace of digital hyper-consumption.

It is precisely, however, in relation to the question of the superego that the greatest difference between Stiegler's and Lacan's perspectives emerges. Lacan had portrayed the superego exclusively in its Freudian orientation as a "pure culture of the death instinct," seeing in it only an injunction to enjoy that torments the subject in its identification with parental objects whose desires are inevitably at odds with those of the child herself. Stiegler emphasizes instead that aspect of the superego which organizes the capacity for idealization and for the projection of ideal possibilities onto a consistent horizon that will become a future, and according to which life can be experienced as worth living (that aspect being the ego ideal, as discussed in Chapter 1). The superego, which Stiegler charges psychoanalysis with having not yet adequately thought (2014, p. 10), is not to be thought solely on the basis of a reflexive self-punitiveness. Instead, the superego must be thought as the effect of the relationship between the generations, and in terms of which tradition is constituted not only as a relation to the values of the past, but as the projection of a future in which what *does not yet* exist can come into being. Justice is Stiegler's privileged example of that which *does not exist,* and which can never exist concretely, but which *consists* on an order of experience that appears "spiritual" (or "spectral," in Derridean terms), and in such a way that organizes human behavior in the form of a *limit* that retroactively bestows upon experience and behavior an orientation toward community that achieves a complexity deserving of the name of *politics* as a technical, historical practice of individuation. What is called politics today has been reduced to managerial strategies that are embarrassingly undeserving of this name.

What *Antigone*—and Antigone, herself—speaks to is the tendency toward regression inherent to this process. In defying Creon, Antigone does not oppose an enemy from whom she absolutely distinguishes herself. Creon is recognizably driven by his own desires, which is to say his own desire having regressed to the level of the drives as an expression of narcissism having become the articulation of the communal good. Creon is the figure of *fundamentalism* in this sense. Antigone, however, rather than being purified of the position of the desiring subject in upholding the laws of the divine, rigorously commits to this position even more than her adversary. She is, in this way, no less basely driven in her efforts to bury the Thing that is her sublime filial love for Polynices. What Heidegger, Lacan and Stiegler all recognize is that Antigone is in no way in a position of superiority or purity with regard to the

Antigone 97

gerontological tyrant that she defies. With and in her being—which is a process of adolescence or of becoming-mature—she discloses a *violent fundamentalism of justice*.

Against Creon, which to say *with* him as a mirror of his own failures as a leader, Antigone invokes a memory of the gods as the consistency of a law that supersedes anything for which the order of the state, of logic as the law of the collective, and as embodied by Creon, might attempt to justify: "Zeus created these laws, not you," she insists, in defiance of an elder who has forgotten this difference. In transgressively sublimating (individuating) herself by means of her commitment to fidelity to the status of the Thing, Antigone does nothing to justify her actions—her gestures have nothing to do with the projection of justice (*dikē*) on what Stiegler would call a plane of consistency, which again does not exist in any ordinary sense but which animates the actions of human beings in ways that bring them together in the form of communities that experience themselves as such to the extent that they have a distant, "spectral" sense that ideas and values are *shared*. *Antigone* is about the breakdown of this process, in which the projection of social values becomes something that belongs only to a community bound—unstably and entropically—by its narcissistic commitments.

This is the sense in which a community—as an institution of the difference or *différance* that both separates and connects the generations—has a future. Following Derrida's now famous remark in *Of Grammatology* (1976, p. 5), Stiegler regards this future as a *monstrosity* that cannot be anticipated, and that as result both bears and projects the traces of both a sublime idealism and a tragic fate. For deconstruction, this undecidable future is the Thing that is not an object, that consists but that does not exist, having achieved a dignity that is neither the object of desire nor of the drive, but of the *to-come* (*l'a-venir*) that must be organized on a materialist basis and incessantly practiced upon, by contributing so as to constitute the public domain by cultivating practices of *reading* and *writing*. Writing is in this sense, from the perspective of deconstruction, the essence of sublimation as transgression, as an effort to create new social values by defying authority to the point of affirming insistently the limit of death. This is what Stiegler saw in the advent of what he had called "tertiary retention," which Derrida had indicated by the evolutionary appearance of what he had called the trace as the externalization of tendencies toward self-organization, which Freud, beginning in 1920, had called Eros.

★★★

What can be witnessed in reading Heidegger, Lacan and Stiegler together in this manner, as facilitated by their shared commitment to an appreciation of *Antigone* as central to an experience of what it means to belong to the Western tradition, which begins with the Greeks who we are struggling— and failing, *badly*—to inherit today, is an understanding of the process of development to which each human being is subjected in its relation to

98   *Antigone*

death as a limit that makes development, transformation and therapeutic change fundamental possibilities. This process is not in any way historically stable; it must be constantly negotiated in such a way that this negotiation is what the relationship between the generations *is,* as Freud has attempted to articulate in offering a theory of what he called the superego which, as ego ideal, is what generates a sense of tradition that both informs and is the product of the inscription of a written law whose letter is always open in that it must be interpreted. This interpretation is the violence-doing that Heidegger had described as the "essential trait" of Da-sein (the as-structure of being), that Lacan had witnessed in the concept of sublimation as an act of fundamental transgression, and that Stiegler, following Derrida, had thought as *writing* as a materialist practice of "spiritual" individuation in the constitution of desire from out of a tendency toward regression to a baseless economy of the drives that is everywhere being exploited and exhausted today.

In other words, we are currently in an era in which we find ourselves, as Lacan said, "screwed." Thought together, fundamental ontology, psychoanalysis and deconstruction provide the site of a possible path forward.

Notes

1 Recall that, in Chapter 3, we saw Bollas describing what he called the aesthetic moment as constituting a "deep rapport between subject and object, and provid[ing] the person with a generative illusion of *fitting with an object*, evoking an existential memory" (1978, p. 385; emphasis added). Heidegger is using justice in its original Greek sense as an arrangement in precisely this way, so as to indicate that this "fitting" must be *prior* to a metaphysical logic of opposition between mind and world *qua* subject and object. This is why such a fit can only be evoked "existentially," never cognitively, and which would account for its uncanniness, the experience of which we flee from or defend against.
2 "This pervasive sway becomes no less overwhelming because humans take up this sway itself directly into their violence and use this violence as such. This merely conceals the uncanniness of language, of passions, as that into which human beings as historical are disposed (*gefügt*), while it seems to them that it is *they* who have them at their disposal (*verfügt*). The uncanniness of these powers lies in their seeming familiarity and ordinariness. What they yield to humans immediately is merely the inessential, and thus they drive humans out and keep them out of their own essence. In this way, what at bottom is still more distant and more overwhelming than sea and earth becomes something that seems to humans to be the nearest of all" (Heidegger 2000, pp. 166–167).
3 "But to begin with, what is the possibility we call sublimation? Given the time at our disposal, I am not in a position to take you through the virtually absurd difficulties that authors have encountered every time they have tried to give a meaning to the term 'sublimation'" (Lacan 1992, pp. 143–144).

References

Bollas, C. (1978). "The Aesthetic Moment and the Search for Transformation." *Annual of Psychoanalysis*, 6:385–394.

Heidegger, M. (1996a). *Being and Time*. Trans J. Stambaugh. New York: SUNY Press.

Heidegger, M. (1996b). *Hölderlin's Hymn "The Ister"*. Trans. W. McNeil and J. Davis. Bloomington, IN: Indiana University Press.

Heidegger, M. (2000). *Introduction to Metaphysics*. Trans. G. Fried and R. Polt. New Haven, CT: Yale University Press.

Lacan, J. (1992). *The Ethics of Psychoanalysis*. Ed. J.-A. Miller. Trans. D. Porter. New York: W.W. Norton & Company.

Stiegler, B. (2013). *Uncontrollable Societies of Disaffected Individuals*. Trans. D. Ross. New York: Polity.

Stiegler, B. (2014). *The Lost Spirit of Capitalism*. Trans. D. Ross. New York: Polity.

Stiegler, B. (2020). *La leçon de Greta Thunberg. Qu'appelle-t-on panser?: 2*. Paris: Éditions les Liens qui libèrent.

Themi, T. (2014). *Lacan's Ethics and Nietzsche's Critique of Platonism*. New York: SUNY Press.

5 Weapons

> Self control is containing the impulse to run around naked and screeching and biting peoples' faces off.
>
> —Jayalalita devi dasi devi dasi 2016

This final chapter attempts to recover everything discussed so far in the previous chapters into an account of the political stakes of the survival of the psychoanalytic clinic today, to the extent that it functions as a transitional space for the cultivation of symbolizing processes and the work of sublimation under crushing conditions of environmentally enforced *desymbolization* and *desublimation*. My title refers to what a series of thinkers—beginning with Nietzsche—imagined thought must become in order to survive these conditions. According to the philosopher Peter Sloterdijk (2012),

> in real thinking, thoughts belong more closely to their fellow thoughts than the thinker to the world around him … Thinking creates an artificial autism that isolates the thinker and takes him to a special world of imperatively connected ideas. (pp. 28–29)

In the analytic literature, it is Bollas who has understood so well how this *solitude,* which is the condition of real thinking, is being destroyed today, and with it the perceived efficacy of the psychoanalytic clinic. The Freudian practices of free association and evenly hovering attention are attempts to recover this space and time, in which the unconscious is intermittently brought into unconcealment by giving free reign to the connections *between* thoughts, rather than by uncritically accepting the express intentions of the subject. Like dreaming, such thinking requires a solitude at odds with the imperatives of the market-driven world that is intent on absolutely manipulating and thereby inadvertently undermining the cultivation of individual and collective desire (cf. Crary 2013).

More importantly, as Stiegler emphasizes, this solitude is not the result of a naturally occurring development; it must be nurtured—in *both* children

DOI: 10.4324/9781003243878-5

*and*adults—via procedures of thoughtful caregiving. Like the work of psycho-analysis, critical thought is a disciplined effort to open up and to provide such a solitary space: "Life in the secession through thinking owes its existence to the distancing techniques people use to transport themselves to the special zone of theory" (Sloterdijk 2012, p. 80). Far from being an abstraction divorced from the immediacy of lived experience, the "special zone of theory" is an inter-mediary zone between thought and practice—a transitional space, in the most rigorously Winnicottian sense. Analysts who fail at grasping this—those who continue naively (metaphysically) to oppose theory and practice—will miss the revolutionary potential of the clinic in a contemporary cultural and political context, as well as the unique status of psychoanalysis as a science.[1]

Nihilism

In a brief statement made one month into the COVID-19 pandemic, in April 2020, Stiegler invited us to regard confinement as a gift. Drawing on his own experience of confinement following his incarceration for a series of bank robberies in the late 1970s, Stiegler argued that confinement can provide us with a much-needed opportunity for reflection, and to reconnect with practices of traditional care and education—practices everywhere threatened by the destruction of intergenerational connectedness. "Confinement," he wrote, "can revive the memory and meaning of past ways of life" (2020, p. 2). His hope appears to have been that in quarantine and confinement we might find the ability to think again, and to rethink what it means to be able to be and to do things together.

Four months later, Stiegler killed himself. Apparently, he was very sick, with an unspecified illness for which he had long been undergoing hospita-lization. But in his late writings, he had also increasingly become open about a lifetime spent struggling with depression. Having written so extensively from a contemporary Nietzschean perspective, he must have known that his final decision and gesture would not be taken lightly by those familiar with his work.

It must also not have escaped Stiegler that his suicide following a period of protracted illness would appear as a repetition of the final gesture of another great French Nietzschean philosopher: Gilles Deleuze. Deleuze spent the last years of his life like so many under COVID: on a ventilator. Eventually, he threw himself out a window.

I was living in Paris as a student of philosophy when Deleuze committed suicide. He had spent his career criticizing the intrinsically suicidal tendencies of our contemporary world. I still have my copy of the French newspaper *InfoMatin* from that day, which announced on its cover, alongside his photo, "*Gilles Deleuze définitivement hors système.*" I've always thought that headline was hysterically funny, and that Deleuze would have thought so, too.

But the headline had missed the point of Deleuze's work, which was also consistently Stiegler's point, as it was central to Nietzsche's thought:

102 *Weapons*

The world today is one in which there is no "outside the system," no vantage point from which to resist this suicidal trajectory in which we are all killing ourselves in some way or another. Inventing such an advantage would require that our concept of *world* be transformed, and with it the classical notion of *resistance*. To insist that there is "no outside" is not a nihilistic gesture of resignation, nor is it a wink to the new aesthetics of totalitarianism; it is rather an affirmation of the fact that today, to be inside *is* to be outside, and that we must evolve sophisticated strategies of combat in order for life—as the *struggle* for life—to continue to articulate itself.

When Nietzsche's writing is rehearsed within an academic context, we fail to see just how prophetic he was in anticipating the moment through which we are currently living, and the nightmare toward which we are barreling. Nihilism, which means that human beings "rather will *nothingness* than not will" (1967, p. 97; emphasis in original), is a form of psychosis, and the more psychotic psychosis becomes the less it is capable recognizing itself as such. What Nietzsche called nihilism is an illness that relentlessly feeds off of itself in an ever-accelerating way to the point of destroying itself in an absolutely spectacular fashion: "Nothing burns one up faster than the affects of *ressentiment*. Anger, pathological vulnerability, impotent lust for revenge, thirst for revenge, poison-mixing in any sense ... such affects involve a rapid consumption of nervous energy" (1967, p. 230). No philosopher could be more pertinent to our time than Nietzsche because we are far down this path into collective illness, as demonstrated by the fact that for most people, caught up as they are in their own self-destructive behaviors, this decline is virtually unwitnessable. Nietzsche witnessed this unwitnessability, and it eventually destroyed him.

In *The Will to Power* (1968), Nietzsche writes that nihilism is, "the radical repudiation of value, meaning, and desirability" (p. 7). This radical repudiation, become global and systemic today, is not the abandonment of previously and traditionally spiritual principles; it is an organized and dynamic, material practice that undermines the cultivation of desire in the course of every individual's development—desire being the basis for any experience of value and meaning. This process is materialist because, as Nietzsche was the first to understand so well, apparently spiritual principles are rooted in the body and the drives, which in order to function in ways that support the constitution of future horizons that we call ideals, must actively be organized by educational and disciplinary procedures that form the basis of what have traditionally been called cultural institutions. Such organizational efforts—both at the individual and collective levels—are what Nietzsche, following Goethe, and in anticipation of Freud, called sublimation.

It was never the case for Nietzsche, as those who would misrepresent him as a proponent of conservative values would have it, that nihilism consists in a *loss* of traditional values and the spread of liberal, socialist ideals. What is at stake in grasping the generalized effects of the systemic "growth of the desert" is rather the intrinsic capacity of horizontally projective, guiding valuations *to devaluate themselves*, and in such a way that dissimulates this process by portraying this self-devaluation as a form of *progress*: "Toward a characterization of 'modernity.'—Overabundant development of intermediary forms; atrophy of types; traditions break off, schools; *the overlordship of the instincts* ... after the will to power, the willing of ends *and* means, has been weakened" (1968, p. 48; emphases modified). The "overlordship of the instincts" is the demand for immediate drive gratification, itself elevated to the position of an ideal today (i.e., the accumulation of wealth solely for the purpose of unrestricted consumption), which actively works to undermine itself at every turn. Nihilism, for Nietzsche, is not a question of some nostalgic, Spenglerian narrative concerning the "decline of the West," but of the transformation of our capacity to project a sustainable future into a perverse insistence on projecting a future that is explicitly and recognizably unsustainable: "Radical nihilism is the conviction of an absolute untenability of existence when it comes to the highest values one recognizes" (p. 9).

This is why—and again, this is what separates Nietzsche's thinking from all forms of reactionary ideology—nihilism does not constitute a loss of traditional values and a descent into postmodern relativism: "Against 'meaninglessness' on the one hand, against moral value judgements on the other" (p. 7). Transforming themselves from an object of idealizing efforts into something that must be attacked and devalued, the highest metaphysical values of the past become what drive the pursuit of a generalized will to destruction. This describes a loss of responsibility that programs adults to become like children, so that at a historical level actual children are increasingly being raised by adults who more and more are capable of functioning only in an immature manner—the parent becoming more like a friend, undermining the child's capacity to *make* friends. For Nietzsche, nihilism is not the fading of the intrinsically valuable ideals of the traditional past into something crass and vulgar. Nihilism names rather the inauguration of a new tradition that works actively to attack the very possibility of the emergence of any sustainable future horizon. This is why modernity, as Nietzsche sees it, is not a *fall into* metaphysics but the ultimate and epochal *realization of* metaphysics: "The nihilistic consequence (the belief in valuelessness) as a consequence of moral valuation" (p. 11).

The week I sat down to sketch out the initial outline of what would become this chapter began with massive outrage over a "viral" video of an unarmed man being shot in the back seven times at point blank range in front of his children by a police officer. The monstrous injustice of this act aside, what was so striking was that this occurred in the middle of months of unrest that began with the murder of George Floyd, and soon after that the murder of Rayshard Brooks—events which were themselves captured in videos that also quickly went viral. In no way did the officer who shot Jacob Blake grasp in advance that his act obviously would be captured on video and therefore go viral as well, making a terrible situation even worse, escalating tendencies toward mindless rage which he himself had instanced by going absolutely crazy

104   *Weapons*

in that moment, pulling the trigger *seven times at point blank range*. This unbridled mania and panic is what Nietzsche meant by nihilism.

The next night it is reported that the riots in Kenosha, Wisconsin—which follow this new viral incident, but which are part of a greater historical process—have finally produced the first murders committed by civilians against other civilians. At first, it is not clear what this involves, or to which side the perpetrator belongs. Then, it is announced that a seventeen-year-old boy with an assault rifle who dreamt of one day becoming a police officer has been arrested and is charged with two counts of intentional homicide. He is part of a group of armed citizens who had come from out of state to protect private property, hoping to assist trained adults who were incapable of doing so themselves.

As cell phone videos of the events that took place in Kenosha begin to emerge and to circulate, the chubby child who identified with the law—but in such a way that encouraged him to act out his violent fantasies—and the group to which he belongs are aggressively denounced over the ensuing hours as "virulent" racists. *The New York Times* constructs a narrative of events based on these videos, and the article it publishes generates a comments section which draws over 1800 responses (indicating a much vaster, widespread readership) in which virtually everyone denounces the violence of the right and sees racism as the greatest illness of our time. No one questions the perspective they have internalized; instead, they proudly announce their conviction that it would be crazy not to see that it is the other side that is to blame. Mistaking the symptom for the illness is the illness that Nietzsche called nihilism.

As all of this transpires, nightly television programming is dominated by the spectacle of the Republican National Convention, in which an illiterate gameshow host and his followers insist that this increasingly violent world over which he presides can be blamed on his opponent and that the only cure for this violence is his reelection because what is happening now threatens to become the future and to spread virally everywhere as it has under his own administration, for which he assumes no responsibility. He promises to cure us of society's ills, just as he had cured us of the spread of COVID-19, which is treated as a thing of the past, as the national death toll rises quickly toward 200,000, and as it will eventually surpass 500,000. Each of his children attests to the magical powers of their father, captivating viewers. This tendency toward uncontrollable captivation is also what Nietzsche called nihilism.

How is one to think affirmatively under these conditions? For Nietzsche, affirmation necessarily involves experimentation, which is another way in which to think the concept of sublimation (1996, pp. 12–13). The need for experimentation issues from the insight that, "there are no eternal facts, just as there are no absolute truths" (p. 13). In the absence of immutable, objective truths, what is required is interpretation as a form of "*historical philosophizing.*" The degradation of the capacity to think in such a way is what the spread of nihilism is predicated upon: "This same species of man, grown one stage poorer, no longer possessing the strength to interpret, to create fictions, produces *nihilists*" (1968, pp. 317–318; emphasis in original). To interpret the sensible and the intelligible is to create fictions—to *fictionalize*—in order to create new ideals, to revaluate all values.

"According to Heidegger's interpretation of Nietzsche's thought," writes Franco Berardi (2015), "the absence of a metaphysical truth, and the consequent lack of objectively existing moral values, confers the responsibility of knowledge and moral choice to the act of interpretation, and to the act of will" (p. 87). This is what it means to philosophize historically, without any underlying ground or law that would guarantee the results. This is what Heidegger called ground as openness, which is why Berardi describes this program as a form of "hermeneutic nihilism":

> This form of nihilism assumes that the conceptual activity is based on the ontological *nihil*. In this conception, this form of nihilism has a positive and constructive implication, as the condition of moral freedom and of conceptual creation. *Nihil* is the starting point of the conceptual and practical process, and from this starting point the conceptual and historical activity of men is responsible for the creation and meaning of the world as we know it. (pp. 87–88)

Hermeneutic nihilism is not the nihilism Nietzsche decries; it is the positive embrace of ground as openness that Heidegger had described as the terrifying, uncanny *freedom* of Da-sein—*prior* to its determination in the form of any given, socially figured and therefore infinitely defensible identity. Responsibility precedes identity and the demand for personal recognition. In contrast,

> The form of nihilism that seems to prevail in the culture and practice of the ruling class today is quite different from this constructive, hermeneutic nihilism. We could call it a form of 'annihilating nihilism,' since it actively produces *nihil* as its effect. (ibid.)

The production of nothing is not only annihilating (in that it produces annihilation), it demonstrates the difference between production and creativity that Nietzsche insists our modern world works not only to conceal but to exploit to the point of exhaustion. To *live* creatively or experimentally can only appear opportunistic where production is no longer thought in terms of the production of symbols, but exclusively in terms that serve a marketplace in which exchange has been thoroughly abstracted or financialized—as an exchange of empty promises rather than of symbolic *goods*. This is the annihilating nihilism that undermines creativity without, unlike in earlier eras, opening new possibilities for creative resistance. Kierkegaard (1962) spoke of this when he described our era as one defined by the death of rebellion:

> A revolutionary age is an age of action; ours is the age of advertisement and publicity. Nothing ever happens but there is immediate publicity

106   *Weapons*

everywhere. In the present age a rebellion is, of all things, the most unthinkable. Such an expression of strength would seem ridiculous to the calculating intelligence of our times ... Equally unthinkable among the young men of today is a truly religious renunciation of the world, adhered to with daily self-denial. (p. 6)

The present age with its sudden enthusiasm followed by apathy and indolence is very near the comic; but those who understand the comic see quite clearly that the comic is not where the present age imagines. Now satire, if it is to do a little good and cause immeasurable harm, must be firmly based upon a consistent ethical view of life, a natural distinction which renounces the success of the moment; otherwise the cure will be infinitely worse than the disease ... What, indeed, is there for an age of reflection and thought to defy with humour? For, being without passion, it has lost all feeling for the values of eros, for enthusiasm and sincerity in politics and religion, or for piety, admiration and domesticity in everyday life. (p. 10)

Religion, in Kierkegaard's terms, reflects the cultivation of interiority by means of renunciation and self-denial as disciplinary techniques of individuating *autopoiesis*. The care of the self (to put it in Foucault's terms) is the cultivation of passion and desire as against the "leveling process" that results in "an age without passion [that] has no values, [where] everything is transformed into representational ideas" (p. 11). With the death of rebellion, which is death (*nihil*) itself as the apathetic renunciation of life as struggle,

The springs of life, which are only what they are because of the qualitative differentiating power of passion, lose their elasticity. The distance separating a thing from its opposite in quality no longer regulates the inward relation of things. All inwardness is lost, and to that extent the relation no longer exists, or else forms a colourless cohesion. (p. 15)

For both Kierkegaard and Nietzsche, this is the sickness of our age, one that consists in an annihilating nihilism which precludes interpretation as symbolization and as the ability to create fictions, reducing everything everywhere to the operational management of desymbolized, concrete facts: information without in-formation ("the inward relation of all things"). Suicide as a result becomes an uncontrollable imperative, though one drawn out over the course of an unlived lifetime consumed by deliberation and the leveling down of everything to abstract, representational ideas:

Nowadays not even a suicide kills himself in desperation. Before taking the step he deliberates so long and so carefully that he literally chokes with his thought. It is even questionable whether he ought to be called a suicide, since it is really thought which takes his life. He does not die *with* deliberation but *from* deliberation. (p. 3; emphases in original)

Weapons 107

Clearly, there are limits to Kierkegaard's vision here, as Nietzsche was well aware in having foreseen that the coming age would be *extremely violent*, and that suicide would come increasingly to subsume the place and the dynamic of rebellion itself. Embracing nihilism as annihilation in this way is the hallmark of what Nietzsche understood by *weakness*. Weakness, however, is not for Nietzsche something simply opposed to strength—it is *not* the absence of power—just as illness is not opposed to health, but serves as a necessary passage through which the transformation of *ressentiment* (envy) constitutes the most necessary effort at sublimation, which it also engenders and cultivates, in its own insistently destructive way. For Nietzsche, this passage is a *militant* necessity today, one that discloses life as the struggle for life, which Heraclitus had long ago described as a *war*: "War is the father of all and king of all, and some he shows as gods, others as men; some he makes slaves, others free" (Kirk, Raven and Schofield 1983, p. 193). Nietzsche saw in this not an apology for violence, but the irreducibility of conflict as authorizing a certain critical violence in the effort to heal in the cultivation of affirmation, desire and care:

> Freedom from *ressentiment*, lucidity about *ressentiment*—who knows how much I ultimately have to thank my long sickness for these as well! The problem is not exactly a simple one: you need to have experienced it out of strength and out of weakness. If there are drawbacks to being sick and weak, it is that these states wear down the true instinct for healing, which is the human instinct for *weapons and war*. (Nietzsche 2005, p. 80; emphasis in original)

Freud too, being a product of his time, saw the irreducibility of this violence and conflict. For this reason, he linked the struggle for civilization to the superego and to processes of sublimation:

> It is in keeping with the course of human development that external coercion gradually becomes internalized; for a special mental agency, man's super-ego, takes it over and includes it among its commandments. Every child presents this process of transformation to us; only by that means does it become a moral and social being. Such a strengthening of the super-ego is a most precious cultural asset in the psychological field. *Those in whom it has taken place are turned from being opponents of civilization into being its vehicles.* (1927, p. 11; emphasis added)

Those who understand the Freudian superego only as an agency of self-punishment and guilt will read this passage as if Freud were praising that aspect of it, justifying the internalization of coercion despite the misery this inevitably generates. What this reading misses, however, is how Freud at the same time conceives here of the superego as the agency of hope, discipline and the anticipation of a good, desirable future. The internalization of coercion is not

108   *Weapons*

*just*oppression, it is *also* the economizing of the drives as the generation of desire. That is, superego is that structure of mind which both makes possible and is made possible by sublimation, according to which those who are predisposed to *despise* the revolting *stupidity* of civilization today with all of their being, can be provided the opportunity to become cultural contributors. Or not.

War for the control of symbols

In one of his earliest, and what one should hope will prove to be his most enduring texts, Deleuze (1994) wrote,

> ... we believe that when these problems attain their proper degree of *positivity*, and when difference becomes the object of a corresponding *affirmation*, they release a power of aggression and selection which destroys the beautiful soul by depriving it of its very identity and breaking its good will. The problematic and the differential determine struggles or destructions in relation to which those of the negative are only appearances, and the wishes of the beautiful soul are so many mystifications trapped in appearances. The simulacrum is not just a copy, but that which overturns all copies by *also* overturning the models: every thought becomes an aggression. (p. xx; emphases in original)

Decades later, Deleuze would translate this sentiment into a call for the creation of new concepts—which he had from the beginning of his career (Deleuze 1983), following Nietzsche, compared to arrows—in the fight against what he had come to call, echoing William Burroughs, *control societies,* in the midst of which, "It is not a question of worrying or of hoping for the best, but of finding new weapons" (Deleuze 1995, p. 178). A thematics of control was seized upon in this context to indicate our having, toward the end of the twentieth century, surpassed the evolution of disciplinary societies as described by Foucault. Control does not merely displace to the margins but thoroughly eradicates the very possibility of spaces for freedom and resistance, of which creative, critical thought is emblematic. Marcuse (1965) had called this "total administration," and Kierkegaard (1962) had described this over a century before as "the leveling process":

> Enthusiasm *may* end in disaster, but leveling is *eo ipso* the destruction of the individual. No age, and therefore not the present age, can bring the skepticism of that process to a halt, for as soon as it tries to stop it, the law of the leveling process is again called into action. (p. 27; emphasis in original)

Taking up the theme of control, and subjecting this to a genealogy of techniques of control—which requires a genealogy of *technics* (both machine and craft) in general—Stiegler (2014a, 2015) elaborated Nietzsche's theme of nihilism in terms of a *symbolic misery* that pervades all of culture today. This misery is not necessarily depression; it is at the same time a manic energy often channeled toward voracious consumption or, increasingly, violent acts of desperation.

By symbolic misery, Stiegler is not describing an existential mood of our era, but the *immiseration* of our capacities to symbolize and to use symbols, of the symbolic dimension of our lives as this is less and less what culture seeks to cultivate. Where what is cultivated is not achievement but consumer behavior—and no longer merely by inducing hyper-suggestibility but through the *programming* of consciousness at ever younger demographics, displacing primary identifications and replacing these with brand loyalty—processes of individuation become processes of "disindividuation" as overseen by the programming industries, which are the contemporary manifestations of what Horkheimer and Adorno (2007) had been the first to analyze as the "culture industry." Today these industries have moved beyond enforcing domesticity and have insinuated themselves into the developmental processes of human beings generally, depriving them not only of capacities for symbolization and sublimation, but with these the foundations for empathy, attunement and active self-confidence. Generalized programming in this way cultivates an environment of increasing—and increasingly uncontrollable—hostility:

> By symbolic misery I mean … the loss of individuation which results from the *loss of participation* in the *production of symbols*. Symbols here being as much the fruits of intellectual life (concepts, ideas, theorems, knowledge) as of sensible life (arts, know-how, mores). And I believe that the present state of generalized loss of individuation can only lead to a symbolic collapse, or the collapse of desire—in other words to the decomposition of the social as such: to total war. (Stiegler 2014a, p. 10; emphases in original)

The apocalyptic tone of this pronouncement aside, Stiegler is developing a crucial theme in Derrida's work—neglected by "deconstructivists," who by and large seem not to have read much of Derrida, beyond the surface of his occasional stylistic eccentricities—that concerns how the experience and transmission of spiritual abstraction is generated from out of the history of its material inscription. Derrida called this *writing,* expanding the sense of the word.

In *Of Grammatology* (1976), Derrida argued that, contrary to the pre-occupation with linguistics characteristic of his generation and the generation which immediately preceded it, what defined the discourses of the twentieth century—from literature and the arts generally, to theoretical biology and the emergent cognitive and computer sciences—were models of writing, according to a general thematics of *programs* and *programming* that could not admit or conceive of an origin at which these programs (genetic programs, for example) began (Vitale 2018). Rather than conceiving of life in pneumatological terms as the living presence of the spirit or voice, which had been the

110   *Weapons*

tendency of metaphysics at least since Plato up to and including Heidegger, Derrida conceived life as *trace*—as the enigmatic remainder of a life always already past yet still sending itself forward, finitely—upsetting the opposition of the organic and the inorganic, and arguing that life processes are not constrained by or limited to this conceptual opposition. This was, so to speak, a kind of "fourth blow to mankind's narcissism," in that it demonstrated how the evolution of technics has its own speed and evolutionary dynamic, which obviously intersects with, but is ultimately not reducible nor can it be considered secondary to, the dynamics of human evolution.

Like Heidegger, Derrida had seen the destructive potential of major imbalances in the coordination of these two evolutionary dynamics; but like Marx, he was willing to affirm that this fundamental disjunction also contained within itself possibilities for emancipation or at least the promise of future justice. This was the basis for the famously "undecidable" logic that Derrida attempted to work out early on in his career (in many ways following the models of Kurt Gödel in mathematics (Plotnitsky 2002)), and that was symbolized in the notion of the *pharmakon* as both poison and remedy (Derrida 1978).

Stiegler put this notion of the *pharmakon* at the center of his critical approach, comparing it to Winnicott's notion of the transitional object (which is always also the condition of possibility of the fetish and of addiction), and demonstrating via what he called a *pharmacological* analysis that this undecidability is the "de-fault" of essence that the human and the technological (*qua* "organized inorganic matter" (Stiegler 1998)) share, hence their mutually interdependent relationship. In a political context, this was to demonstrate how strategies of resistance are programmed *always* to lapse into totalitarian logics, and that historically this closure risks being final if the metaphysical spirit of humanism is not radically transformed—and not just "today" but *immediately*:

> A thought only has meaning if it has the force of *reopening* the indetermination of a future. But it can only be a matter of new ways of life if those lives are constituted by *new modes of existence*: human life is an existence. Now, our current situation is characterized by the fact that this fails to occur, and that, in place of the necessary creation of these new modes of existence there is substituted an *adaptive* process of *survival*, in which possibilities for existing disappear, being reduced instead to simple modalities of subsistence. (Stiegler 2011, p. 12; emphases in original)

Reducing life to the functions of survival and subsistence, a market that thrives on manipulating the desires of its subjects (as consumers) simultaneously ruins their desire and undermines their capacity for symbolic participation in the world, by depriving them not only of the ability to sublimate so as to constitute desire but also of the knowledge that all previous human generations have transmitted to the present moment. The result of this process—what Stiegler called "proletarianization," as the deprivation of individuals' knowledge of how to live in an industrialized culture no longer limited to the labor market—are generations that will increasingly struggle with not knowing how basically to get by and to find security and stability for themselves, both materially and psychologically.

Bollas, whose "desexualized" account of sublimation—as idiom as unconscious creativity, and as in-formation as unconscious receptivity—we integrated with Loewald's more "classical" (from both a Freudian and a Heideggerian register) thinking in Chapter 3, describes exactly this in discussing the fate of today's younger generation and the difficulties they will transmit to their own offspring, having their ties to the knowledge of the past severely impoverished:

> The "millennials" were born into a world of significantly abbreviated forms of communication, privileging tweets over letters for example. It is a culture generally uninterested in examination of the internal world, enthralled instead with the technologies of apps and networking. They are unlikely to have much awareness of what had been lost to Western consciousness in the decades before their birth … [Yet] forms of loss, states of grief or revenge for the lost can be inherited through acts of unconscious identification. New generations can feel, with a jaded unease, that the promises made by their society, whether explicit or implicit, are not being delivered. (Bollas 2018, p. xi)

Like Stiegler, Bollas thinks this inheritance not as the passing on of mere information from one generation to the next, but as the historical articulation of both individual and collective psychic structures (libidinal economies) that determine ways of being-in-the-world as being-with. The disruptions of this process that define our current world deprive individuals of their individuality—and not by simply oppressing them, but by undercutting processes of psychological development at their very bases:

> Unlike instincts, affects or memories, these patterns of thought are not endogenous formations responsive to intrapsychic forces; they are mentalities promoted by contemporary culture to which the ego will create adaptations. They therefore lack the complex interlacing imbrication of a self's profoundly idiosyncratic psychodynamic. However, although they are developed primarily within social psychology rather than being driven from the depths of individual psychic life, they may eventually become permanent structures in our mind. The price of civilization now is that selves are dominated less by a superego than by an ego that diminishes internal capabilities through deeply compromised forms of thinking. (Bollas 2018, p. 68)

Adaptation here, as both Bollas and Stiegler describe it, is passive conformity to environmental demand *in the absence of any awareness that this is taking place*, given that the relation to the historical past—as that which *links* the

112 *Weapons*

generations, which is *also* what separates them—has been pathogenically compromised. For Bollas, purely adaptive selves "are dominated less by a superego than by an ego that diminishes internal capabilities through deeply compromised forms of thinking." For Stiegler, it is the absence of the superego as it has been traditionally constructed, and as it is increasingly being reconstructed by advertising and marketing departments' control of the production of symbolic ideals (and thus of the horizon of the future, translated as endless consumption), that drives the ego today to diminish itself. As a result,

> The oppressed self must find compromised forms of expression, so that oppression emerges as a new form of being. The drive to return the repressed to consciousness can lead to intriguing symptoms, dreams, linguistic formulations and even artistic creations, but a self who is suffering from profound oppression will reveal impoverishments of thinking and affect. This can be understood as a form of mental suicide, or subjecticide, which offers the self an ego position in the new social order through the elimination of sophisticated forms of perception and thoughtfulness. (Bollas 2018, pp. 68–69)

In Bollas's example of the millennial generation exchanging written letters for character-limited text messages, and individuated interiority for social networking—and in doing so for unstoppable reasons far beyond their control, a fact which as a result increasingly no longer concerns them—this situation most clearly reveals the war over the production and control of symbols in which we are all now immersed (Stiegler 2014a, p. xiii). This is a war that must be fought with new weapons because it occurs not as (spiritual, political) *polemos*, but at the level of *programming*, both of the body and the mind today. The culture industries, having become the programming industries, are now the main instruments in the management of "attention economies," which systematically destroy attention, and thus ultimately themselves.

Stiegler sees this war over the control of symbols and thus over the fate of individuals *as* individuals as the outcome of what he calls, following Derrida, *grammatization*: a process inherent to both organic and inorganic (technical) life, in terms of which the relationship between these entangled organizations of matter reciprocally and dynamically in-form one another over the course of millennia, producing both recorded history and the experience of history by inscribing in each new generation, and at the level of each individuated, discrete (grammatized) psyche, a memory of a past never lived but inherited through primary identifications. The disruption of this process constitutes a new contemporary epoch of this process, which has begun to operate as a *war against itself*:

> The process of grammatization is the basis of political power understood *as the control of the process of psychic and collective individuation. The hyperindustrial age is characterized by the development of a new stage in the process of*

grammatization, now extended, in the discretization of gesture, behavior and movement in general, to all kinds of spheres, going well beyond the linguistic horizon. This is also what constitutes Foucault's bio-power—which is simultaneously control of consciousness.

But, since the unconscious cannot be controlled, the control society is a censorship society of a new kind which is unavoidably incubating an *explosion of drives*—preceded by myriad forms of variously soothing compensatory discourse. Here, where it is not a matter of fearing or hoping, but of 'finding new weapons,' that is, of *fighting* … (Stiegler 2014a, p. 57; emphases in original)

Bollas describes this same form of censorship society, which is not a society of repression as typically described by Freud. What is at issue in new forms of directive censorship that crystallize over the course of the twentieth century and that have become fully realized today is not the effort to suppress thoughtful content, but a globally systemic attempt to control being:

At this [Freud's] time—indeed from the previous century—other forms of censorship were gathering mass and structure. This was a censorship organized, not against unacceptable ideas, but against the self's right to *be*. Oppression came in many forms and histories: the poverty of the working class; the subordinating of women and children; the domination of countries by leaders who sent millions to their deaths in the "cumulative trauma" of war after war; the assimilation of human beings into the forces of capitalism that overrode the rights of the individual. Although Freud's view of oppression was initially localized to inner censorship, in *Civilization and Its Discontents*, written after the Great War, he turns to a different conflict: the one between the demands of society and the urges of the self. (Bollas 2018, p. 34; emphasis in original)

What Bollas ignores, as always, is that for Freud, the "urges of the self" are primarily sexual urges. In *Civilization and Its Discontents,* Freud is concerned with emergent forms of civilization as structures linking individual and social libidinal economies according which the drives of the individual are organized by, so as to be capable of being channeled through, social circuits of identification that can provide meaningful bases for opportunities "to love and to work." The "pessimistic" tone of *Civilization and Its Discontents* is determined by Freud's perception that civilization is evolving in such a way as no longer to do this, but instead to promote a "strange attitude of hostility to civilization" (1930, p. 38)—a hostility toward itself. The Great War that preceded the appearance of Freud's text, and the next Great War which Freud clearly discerns as the horizon of his time, were early symptoms of the unthinkably disastrous war that civilization was on track not only to fight but to become: a total war that is a zero-sum game.

114   *Weapons*

What must be fought against is this total war itself. This requires new weapons because it is not a political fight but a fight *for politics*, which is at the same time a fight for the internal space of reflection and symbolic understanding, as well as empathy, desire and care.[2] If there are names for an enemy here, they would be *populism* (as the opposite, which is to say the most degenerate form, of politics) and *positivism* (in the sense of fact-minded, de-symbolizing concreteness). These two quasi-political and quasi-psychological formations could be further reduced and integrated under the heading of *fundamentalism* as a structure not just of mind but of being, which is to say irrespective of the particular contents of the ideals to which this structure finds itself arbitrarily attached at any given moment.

What appears now as symbolic misery, producing nihilism in its manic phase, will be superseded—*if* anything survives, but not if everything that survives knows *only how* to survive—by what can only be conceived as an inhumanity. Inhumanity is something quite different from a void, which still constitutes an abstract ideal and thus, for the most desperate among us, continues to emanate hope. Inhumanity, on the other hand, would be worse than *nihil*, as a life without life, of beings absolutely synchronized in the grammar of their being, which is to say without any remainder of unconscious processes:

> The exteriorization of human memory [i.e., writing, in Derrida's expanded sense], which has allowed for the accumulation and transmission of individual experiences, would end up in the creation of a reactive network, as though this experience were from now on entirely standardized and disembodied. With this hypothesis, the man-technic coupling would only have needed individual liberty—over a few thousand years—in order for the system to develop correctly and form a 'supra-individual organism' which, at the moment of its total planetization, ultimately resembles that of the *perfectly synchronous* organization of what we call social insects. (Stiegler 2014a, pp. 77–78; emphasis in original)

Such synchronization could only occur from out of the absolute reduction of time as the organizational principle of psychic structure (Loewald), which would be the remainder or trace of our having dispensed with even the most rudimentary forms of enviro-somatic caregiving (Bollas), according to which the screen functionally replaces the parent. This is entirely within the realm of possibility today. In contrast, socialization still,

> consists in a unifying synchronization that one can always also analyze as domination and polemical (eristic) diachronization, wherein singularities are formed as the *sublimation* of war—thus as the sublime expression of the worst becoming the best. Such an analysis demands ... that we try to understand the question of reason—and to understand it *anew, that is*, as motive, mobility, design, and beyond *ratio*, on which this question has run aground. (Stiegler 2011, p. 52; emphases in original)

Reason having become *ratio*—what Max Weber (2012) had called *rationalization*, in a sense different from, though not unrelated to, Freud's use of the term—is thought reduced to calculation. Heidegger had extensively taken up this theme but had consistently made the mistake of *opposing* thought and *ratio* (as poetic and calculative thinking, for instance (Heidegger 1969)), whereas what must be critically appreciated today is the way in which these tendencies mutually depend upon and implicate one another. This is why Stiegler privileges psychoanalysis in that it provides a thinking of libidinal economy as what irreducibly links the individual and the political, even in or as an attitude of hostility. From an analytic perspective, hostility to civilization can still function as a form of civilized participation and contribution. At the same time, participation and contribution can occur in a thoroughly uncivilized and destructive manner. This is what worried Freud in 1930.

Ecstatic violence—from *Fight Club* to *Iron Gates*

Before returning to the question of the clinic as a weapon in the fight for a less monstrous, less inhuman future, we would do well to linger a while longer on the present, on the mania of what Nietzsche had called active nihilism, which still demonstrates a preference for "willing *nothingness*, rather than not willing at all." The evolution of this preference over the past several generations, and the pace at which it keeps redoubling itself, provides a disturbing lesson in how breakdowns in the relationships between the generations manage to amplify rather than to transform each generation's pathologies, and continuously to efface the boundaries between fantasy and reality, which erodes the power to create fictions.

Like most Westerners, at least since the 1960s, I grew up under a cultural injunction that encouraged the idealization of suicidal drug addicts: famous musicians, artists, movie stars, etc., who had died young. While self-destruction has always held a romantic appeal for youth, it was not until the late 1960s that such figures were embraced and promoted in their very self-destructiveness by the culture industries. By the time this marketing campaign had reached my generation—called "X" because, presumably, unlike the generations before and after us, we were immune to marketing strategies designed to instill brand loyalty (this was most certainly not true, or if it was then the problem has since been solved by the marketing of "retro" culture to the adolescents of the nineties who are now in their forties and fifties)—it had evolved to a point at which it had begun to lose control. The result was that the figure emblematic of romantic youth with which my generation was encouraged to identify had not pursued the tragic path to symbolic immortality via accidental drug overdose. Instead, in a calculated effort to guarantee the endurance of his brand, he deliberately committed suicide with a shotgun, at the appropriate, pre-determined age (i.e., "Club 27").[3]

For many of us who at the time saw through and were unimpressed with this sadly depressing program, we were left not with a sense of overwhelming

116   *Weapons*

symbolic loss but with an even stronger conviction that popular culture had nothing to offer, and that to choose anything it did have to offer would be self-destructive. Self-destructiveness was something we were at the same time becoming no longer completely opposed to, without realizing it.

In 1996, this situation changed with the appearance of Chuck Palahniuk's novel *Fight Club*, which quickly became a point of focus among young men between the ages of twenty and thirty who were of the first generation struggling to come to terms with the then-emerging alteration in the human developmental sequence now called "post-adolescence." Leaning not quite as far to the left as our more conventional peers, we found the book exhilarating for its unapologetic celebration of male aggressiveness, and its deeply sensitive appreciation of what it was like to have grown up in a cultural vacuum without the bonds of brotherhood that fighting has traditionally encouraged.

The book also introduced a word into our vocabulary, on the basis of which we were able to distinguish ourselves from those who found the novel to be morally repugnant for its glorified depictions of phallic violence: snowflake. "You are not a beautiful and unique snowflake," Tyler Durden tells his army of "space monkeys" (Palahniuk 1996, p. 134), writing this down and encouraging them to bark it at one another in order to motivate themselves to commit pranks of political violence against corporate anti-culture. This was the most timely portrayal of a desire for both chaos and structure, both discipline and Dionysian revelry.

Three years later, in 1999, when *Fight Club* was made into a major Hollywood motion picture—starring a former underwear model and an Ivy League graduate, playing characters whose primary appeal lay in their acknowledged desire to beat those kinds of people up, in order to level the playing fields of privilege—this word gradually began the process of seeping into mainstream discourse and has since been coopted by those to whom it initially seemed fit to apply: those primarily preoccupied with issues of identity and personal recognition.

1999 was also the year of the massacre at Columbine High School in Colorado. Due to the impact of the violence there, the *Fight Club* film was financially unsuccessful upon release, booed by festival audiences and reviled by critics for being socially irresponsible. Apparently, the movie studio even pressured director David Fincher to remove a scene in which the main character threatens his boss by suggesting that an anonymous someone, "might just snap and then stalk from office to office with an Armalite AR-10 carbine gas powered semiautomatic weapon pumping round after round into colleagues and coworkers." (Much to his credit, and perhaps with an awareness of what Kierkegaard had meant when he wrote, "satire, if it is to do a little good and cause immeasurable harm, must be firmly based upon a consistent ethical view of life," Fincher refused to follow orders.) The bloodshed at Columbine—the murder of children, by children—had brought out into the open a new puritan alliance, leading to condemna-tions of the film, as well as of so much else at the time, by angry and

Weapons 117

opportunistic partisans on both sides of the political spectrum. People generally had become more inclined to identify with the privileged position of the uncomfortable, threatened boss.

In his *Heroes: Mass Murder and Suicide* (2015), Franco Berardi posits the year 1977 as a watershed moment in the evolution of civilized culture. This was the year in which the figure of the hero—the individual who functions as the basis for others' ideals, based on her capacity for disciplined achievement—died, or rather, became something it previously was not. Both the cause and the effect of this turning point, according to Berardi, was the fact that human beings had "lost faith in the reality of life and its pleasures, and started believing only in the infinite proliferation of images" (p. 6). 1977 marked the year that creative ideals like David Bowie became mere idols (like David Bowie), and the appearance of British punk rock provocatively but presciently announced, "NO MORE HEROES!" and "NO FUTURE!" This was the moment at which, "from the age of human evolution the world shifted to the age of de-evolution or de-civilization." For Berardi, and in response to this shift,

> The question now is to see what's left of human subjectivity and sensibility and of our ability to imagine, to create and to invent. Are humans still able to emerge from this black hole; to invest their energy in a new form of solidarity and mutual help? The sensibility of a generation of children who have learned more words from machines than from their parents appears to be unable to develop solidarity, empathy and autonomy. History has been replaced by the endless flowing recombination of fragmentary images. (pp. 6–7)

Dylan Klebold and Eric Harris were too old to have lived their most formative early years under these conditions. They were young enough, however, to have been born into a world without heroes—obsessed instead with celebrity and lacking in either meaningful or realistic ideals. And, unlike those of us experiencing the first historical manifestations of post-adolescence at the time, they were *completely unaware of this fact*. Born into this situation, they could not experience it as a loss. They could only inherit it as a nothing (*nihil*).

The difference—which is at the same time a critical parallel—between 1977 and 1999 was that the Columbine killers had not rejected commercial culture, they had embraced it, having identified with its underlying message more insistently than had been previously imaginable. Nowhere was this more recognizable than in the way they had finally imitated the gesture of self-managed martyrdom that had propelled Kurt Cobain to mythical superstar status just five years earlier:

> A violent acting out, as disconnected from a conscious elaboration of it: *just do it*. Nike's motto is a good introduction to the cycle of depression, catatonia and psychotic acting out that can culminate into spectacular murder suicide. (Berardi 2015, p. 56; emphasis in original)

118   *Weapons*

The massacre Klebold and Harris carried out, however, was not something they *just did*. Not only was it meticulously planned, they *dreamt about it together*—in videos they made prior to the day of the shootings, where they speculated about what the consequences would be beyond their suicidal intentions. Berardi points out that they discussed at one point whether it would be better for the film about their actions to be directed by Quentin Tarantino or Steven Spielberg. These children, like all children today, "wanted to air some message, to become famous, and used video and the internet to give vent to their rage and to broadcast their vision of the world" (p. 44). Like the world their actions were apparently condemning, they sought recognition, notoriety, and ultimately, acceptance on some level.

Winnicott defined psychopathy as the "end-product of deprivation." He described psychopathic personalities as those "persons who, *when hopeful*, must make society acknowledge their deprivation" (1970, p. 139; emphasis in original). As horrific as their actions were, the Columbine killers had expressed a certain kind of hope, in that they dreamt of a future that would be *theirs*—but only in the posthumous circulation of fragmentary images that had become the horizon of a future which they were of the first generation to inherit:

> *Just do it*: violence, explosion, suicide. Killing and being killed are linked in this kind of acting out, although the murderer may, exceptionally, survive. When running amok, the borders between one's body and the surrounding universe are blurred, and so is the limit between killing and being killed. Panic, in fact, is the simultaneous perception of the totality of possible stimulations, the simultaneous experience of everything, of every past, every future. In this state of mental alteration the distinction between the self and the universe collapses. (Berardi 2015, p. 56; emphasis in original)

Berardi's description of this state in which "the distinction between the self and the universe collapses" is striking to the extent that it echoes Loewald's description of primary narcissism, as the experience sought after in relation to Bollas's transformational object. Was Columbine a kind of sublimation, or an effort to access what the capacity for genuine sublimation promises? Yes, if we grant that this massacre—this *apocalypse of children's being*, outbreaks of which are occurring everywhere with ever greater frequency today—took place at the limits of the most desperate nihilism, as an attempt to secure an experience of the sublime no less horrific than the crimes of Antigone and the consequences for the world impacted by her actions.

Fight Club stages this same effort, as the search for an experience beyond that provided by the degradation of life brought on by its reduction to commodity form. In a scene from the novel which did not make it into the film, the narrator first encounters his superego or ego ideal on a nude beach, where he is planting driftwood in the sand, so that at a precise moment the sun will cast shadows of the wood in such a way that resembles an open hand, in the middle of which he sits, as if being held: "The giant shadow hand was perfect for one minute, and for one perfect minute Tyler had sat in the palm of a perfection he'd created himself" (Palahniuk 1996, p. 33). The scene evokes both the sublime and the narrator's desperate search for it: "One minute was enough, Tyler said, a person had to work hard for it, but a minute of perfection was worth the effort. A moment was the most you could ever expect from perfection" (ibid.). The characters in *Fight Club* are all searching for this sublime moment, for which one has to work hard, in which time briefly becomes a space.

This is not, of course, to suggest that all acts of explosive, homicidal-suicidal violence are efforts at sublime transgression. In fact, Berardi's description of this state of panic (from the Greek god *Pan*—the one who causes terror) is less accurate as a description of the state of mind of the Columbine killers than it is of that mass murderer with whom he is more centrally preoccupied throughout the book: James Holmes, who in 2012 murdered twelve and wounded seventy others in Aurora, Colorado. Holmes attacked his victims, which included children as young as six, at a midnight screening of the film *Batman: The Dark Knight Rises* (Nolan 2012), while he himself was dressed up as the character Joker. Berardi writes that, in contrast to the Columbine killers, as well as Virginia Tech's Seung-Hui Cho and Pekka-Erik Auvinen in the Finnish city of Tuusula,

> The Joker James Holmes is different: he both subverted and further developed the relationship between crime and the media. While Harris and Klebold were hoping for Spielberg's attention, Holmes was already mimicking a character from Nolan's movie. Holmes is already part of the world of Batman, reconfiguring Marvel's creation in reality, dissolving the boundary of the screen and forcing the audience to participate in the story that they have chosen merely to watch. (p. 44)

The characters in *Fight Club* attempt to *resist* the spectacle of irrecuperable loss that is the fruitless search for recognition in the marketplace of endless commodification (this is why the first two rules of Fight Club stipulate that one does not talk about Fight Club). Klebold and Harris attempted to *contribute* to this marketplace, to punctuate or put to an end by securing meaning in recognition by acting out historically—that is, in a way that would surely not be overlooked or soon forgotten—and by sending a message that symbolized their desperation. Klebold and Harris were trying to remind us of the importance of intergenerational memory, to express what it means not to be but to feel that one is without parents.

What makes Holmes's crime so much even more disturbing, in contrast, is the extent to which the border between reality and fantasy had been absolutely dissolved, such that there was no message, no effort on the part of the killer to symbolize his inner torment, no search for recognition. Dressed up in Joker makeup, Holmes's moment was one in which time did not become

120 *Weapons*

a space, but rather was reduced to the empty, meaningless *now* of objective presence. The massacre in Aurora, unlike the massacre just thirteen years earlier and only twenty-eight miles away in Columbine, contained no symbolic message but was entirely concrete. In that "he both subverted and further developed the relationship between crime and the media," this is to say that Holmes literally *accomplished nothing*: There was no symbolic link between the *Dark Knight* film and Holmes's crime; the differential separation-connection between reality and fantasy had been thoroughly obliterated. Klebold and Harris had attempted to symbolize the extent to which they felt they had been failed; Holmes simply expressed this failure (*nihil*) itself. This difference describes a situation that is *much more volatile* than if reality and fantasy were merely blurred, or if the real had become only an ironic, postmodern "simulacrum."

It would be easy to object that the events in Aurora were unique, to the extent that the killer was more genuinely psychotic (in a clinical sense) than the others mentioned, that in the catalogue of similarly horrific events this was a marginal case that bears no trace of potential future developments. However, two years after Aurora, and fifteen years after Columbine, a novel appeared that, like Palahniuk's *Fight Club*, immediately began to generate a cult following among highly aggressive, post-adolescent males. In 2014, Martinet Press released *Iron Gates*, its authorship attributed not to any individual but to the menacingly anonymous "Tempel ov Blood" [sic], which suggested an organization rather than any single person. The book became an inspiration for the Neo-Nazi group Atomwaffen, which had originally organized around an appreciation for the book *Siege* by James Mason (1992), who had argued that a war for racial cleansing was possible if only the American Nazi Party would submit to the ideological authority of Charles Manson. Atomwaffen was linked to a series of murders between May 2017 and January 2018, and was condemned by the white supremacy movement—not for its involvement in the murders, but because it was suspected of being a recruitment cell for the British satanist network Order of Nine Angles, which encourages members to infiltrate extremist groups in the search for converts to the occult. Pictures of Atomwaffen members posing next to the slogan "IRON GATES NOW!" continue to circulate online. *Iron Gates* is a lurid—poorly written, but genuinely shocking, even by today's standards—novel set in a post-apocalyptic American landscape controlled by an unnamed militaristic organization dedicated to exercising absolute control over all life for the express purpose of exterminating it as violently as possible. The book champions genocide, sexual sadism, human sacrifice and so forth, in a way that betrays an intention not only to provoke but also to lay claim to an extreme and pseudo-informed political ideology (i.e., "Detritus is trash and it was amongst the purview and job description of the commission to exterminate such trash, to sweep away the past so that the organization and its brutal, future ethic could take hold without any traces of pre-apocalyptic humanitarian contaminant left to mar their historic work" (p. 34)—such juvenile passages are typical of the book). Relentless in its graphic depictions of sexual and political violence, the "hero" of *Iron Gates* is ultimately the unnamed organization itself, in its singular mission to destroy life by maximizing cruelty and deception at every available level. Resistance is routinely ferreted out and eviscerated, and loyalty is overridden everywhere by the capricious whims of sadistic interrogators. In one particularly disturbing passage, members of the organization, intoxicated with industrially synthesized chemical stimulants and deliberately poisonous alcohol, ecstatically celebrate their superiors' vision of an endless ecocidal holocaust:

> Now they had advanced their death machine into an entirely new level and their domination would be unstoppable. 'DEATH!' shouted the armaments official, howling like a madman through a generator-run speaker system. 'DEATH!' screamed the unhinged audience in response. 'DEATH! DEATH! DEATH!'—the chant resounded like the roaring of ten-thousand tigers throughout the metal hangar, sweat pouring down every face in emotional exertion. (p. 81)

Aesthetically, the book darkly articulates Heidegger's (1995) alarmed portrayal of a potential future "worldlessness." What worried Heidegger in this guise is currently championed by the philosophical movement known as speculative realism, which traces its inspiration to the work of Quentin Meillasoux (2009).[4] Philosophically, *Iron Gates* drives home with an unusual ferocity the speculative realist insistence that there is no intrinsic connection between the human and the world, and that meditation on a pre-Kantian metaphysical void (also a central tenet of the Order of Nine Angles—though there is, of course, no actual connection between these groups) possesses a certain saving power in relation to the shortcomings of an alleged anthropocentrism.

What sets *Iron Gates* apart from typical entries in the (increasingly popular) sci-fi subgenre of apocalyptic fiction is not only its refusal to apologize for its profound, unrestrained negativity but its palpable desire to serve as a blueprint for terrorist activity in real life (Martinet Press's website states that they, "remain committed to making available texts that instruct, rather than entertain"). It is no accident that groups such as Atomwaffen have adopted an explicitly fictional novel as a political manifesto and, like James Holmes, conduct themselves according to a post-spectacular logic in which the distinction between reality and fantasy (between actual murder and online posturing) has not only been discredited, but is actively being attacked, without any marketable desire for recognition. For this generation of extreme radicals, incapable of fictionalizing reality but very capable of realizing fiction, there is literally *no future*, and therefore nothing today that either separates or connects their world and ours.

122   *Weapons*

Symbolization and its discontents

Freud writes,

> The feeling of happiness derived from the satisfaction of a wild instinctual impulse untamed by the ego is incomparably more intense than that derived from sating an instinct that has been tamed. The irresistibility of perverse instincts, and perhaps the attraction in general of forbidden things finds an economic explanation here. (1930, p. 79)

It is, in the end, a question of intensity—another concept proposed early on and consistently elaborated by Deleuze (1994) as a weapon in the fight against control.[5] The intensity of the sublime in the act of creation will never "convulse our physical being" (Freud 1930, p. 80) like the unmediated expression of a wild, untamed drive. But Freud is not as pessimistic as he may initially seem. The passage continues:

> Another technique for fending off suffering is the employment of the displacements of libido which our mental apparatus permits of and through which its function gains so much flexibility. The task here is that of shifting the instinctual aims in such a way that they cannot come up against frustration from the external world. In this, sublimation of the instincts lends assistance. One gains the most if one can sufficiently heighten the yield of pleasure from the sources of psychical and intellectual work. When that is so, fate can do little against one. A satisfaction of this kind, such as an artist's joy in creating, in giving his phantasies body, or a scientist's in solving problems or discovering truths, has a special quality which we shall certainly one day be able to characterize in metapsychological terms. At present we can only say figuratively that such satisfactions seem 'finer and higher.' (p. 79)

The "special quality" of joy in creation and discovery is not characterizable in anything but figurative terms (as "finer and higher"), while a proper metapsychological account continues to elude Freud. Nonetheless, he has *hope* that *one day* this will have been achieved, so as better to help stabilize the social imbalance of intensities between destruction and creativity. Perhaps the key lies in grasping how the deferral of immediate gratification, if care-*fully* and care-*givingly* handled, can eventually be cultivated into a sense that "fate can do little against one"—that, no matter what, life is worth living.

In a series of lectures delivered between 1929–1930—just at the moment when Freud was writing *Civilization and Its Discontents*—published later as *The Fundamental Concepts of Metaphysics: World, Finitude, Solitude* (1995), Heidegger passed a seemingly different judgment concerning the illness of our age, though it was not without a certain psychoanalytic resonance:

Weapons 123

> The *mystery* [*Geheimnis*] is lacking in our Dasein, and thereby the inner terror that every mystery carries with it and that gives Dasein its greatness remains absent. The absence of oppressiveness is what fundamentally oppresses and leaves us most profoundly empty, i.e., the *fundamental emptiness that bores us*. This absence of oppressiveness is only apparently hidden; it is rather attested by the very activities with which we busy ourselves in our contemporary restlessness. For in all the organizing and program-making and trial and error there is ultimately a universal smug contentment in not being endangered. (pp. 163–164; emphases in original)

As Heidegger saw it, what is so oppressive today is the very absence of oppressiveness—the oppression of a new kind of freedom identified with predictability that gravely endangers us by providing "a universal smug contentment in not being endangered." Boredom is not meant by Heidegger in an ordinary sense, as uneasiness or malaise (Freud's *das Unbehagen*, which he saw as motivated by unconscious guilt (1930, p. 99), which is what Nietzsche and Kierkegaard called *ressentiment*). To be bored by a *fundamental* emptiness, which is extremely different from simply not knowing how to pass one's time, is to be captivated by objective presence, to be unable to temporalize time or to engage with processes of transformation. This is what Heidegger means by the absence of the inner terror induced by *mystery* (*Geheimnis*—which would translate literally as "homeness," cognate of *Heimlichkeit/Unheimlichkeit*). Fundamental ontological emptiness is what is most out there in the open, where it is forgotten and goes unwitnessed, barely noticeable by anyone.

As a concerted effort to disclose unconscious suffering *as* suffering, the psychoanalytic clinic not only retrieves unconscious content, integrating this into a more flexible and robust sense of self; it can function as a lever for intervening at a more profound level of human existence where new forms of oppression and control are insistently insinuating themselves today, as both Bollas and Stiegler, as well as Nietzsche, Heidegger, Burroughs, Deleuze and Derrida describe. By cultivating capacities for symbolization and for sublimation that have been subject to enforced atrophy due to our total immersion in an overwhelmingly predatory and exploitative environment, psychoanalysis offers a strategy for resisting the pull toward the oblivious self-destruction of illiteracy and consumerism.

Symbolization does not just consist in the production of symbols ("putting things into words"); it also encompasses those processes of autopoietic self-organization that make such production possible, and which can, and perhaps more often than not do, occur in complete silence (quiet, solitude). The analytic frame constitutes a space and time—in which each of these occasionally transitions into becoming the other in the generation of symbolic meaning—that intends to facilitate the emergence of *moments* of profound transformation and structural change. Such moments are, of course, not limited to psychoanalysis, but engaging in an analytic process is an effort to amplify their accessibility and impact by means of disciplined practices of open-ended repetition (i.e, speaking without self-censorship, coming frequently to the same place, at the same times, for a period of unspecifiable length, etc.).

Like Nietzsche, Heidegger associated mystery with anxiety, uncanniness and terror. The boredom of our fundamental emptiness is manifest in our constant business, and today in our addiction to screens. This boredom is not dullness, it is precisely the excitement provided by the endless and pervasive consumption of products, images and social networking relationships. We express this boredom as excitement the moment we hit "like," or the moment we click "buy" when an algorithm anticipates what we just might want. Overcoming the addictive excitement of this pervasive boredom requires a confrontation with that which Loewald and Bollas introduce into psychoanalytic discourse, integrating this with Heidegger's understanding of why thinking at this level of our being is something we avoid (because it is not an experience of beatific oneness, as the humanist tradition insists, but something deeply unsettling), and with Derrida and Stiegler's account of how the technical transformation of matter reciprocally in-forms our humanity, both cultivating resistance and making possible regressions to inhumanity.

To cultivate capacities for symbolization and sublimation is intrinsically an act of resistance to the demands of the marketplace and its discouragement of our creatively developing ourselves and living our lives each in his or her or their own most radically individuated manner. The psychoanalytic clinic today, unlike in the past when it functioned predominantly as an instrument of adaptation to logics of control (particularly in North America), has become a site—as an outside within an inside to which there is no longer any outside in a traditional sense—for the elaboration of *singular* forms of resistance against *ever*-evolving frameworks of control. This is because psychoanalysis constitutes *a belief in the world*.[6] The ecstatic space-time of the clinical frame, as a disclosure of our being-in-the-world as being-with-others, is an in-formational technics of being, and can serve as a means of combatting forms of oppression that we no longer suffer under but that we have been forced to internalize so minutely that we have become incapable of recognizing our frenzied collective suicidal behavior for what it is. This kind of oppression cannot be countered with mere empathy or understanding, because it in-forms and de-forms our capacities for empathy and understanding at their very bases. What is needed in response is an approach that is at once conceptual, critical and clinical.

To this end, I have enumerated a series of "weapons" from both philosophy and psychoanalysis that, gathered together in the way that I have attempted here, provide a way of thinking—both critically *and* clinically, as theory and as practice—our current global situation and its effects at the level of each individual—individuals being those who both suffer from, and contribute to and sustain this increasingly insufferable, extremely volatile situation, whether they know it or not.

I will list these weapons below. This list is not meant to be exhaustive, but to encourage others to develop their own programs.

- Freud's concept of sublimation as the autopoiesis of libidinal economies, which is to say of psychic structures, both individual and collective, as this invokes questions other than those concerning unconscious psychological contents, directly implicating the individual not just in the field of the social but in that of the political today;
- Heidegger's attempt at a retrieval of the question of being, as the interpretive disclosure of Da-sein as openness to world, where the latter provides an alternative to the metaphysical figure of the subject to which psychoanalysis still remains uncritically committed;
- Loewald's understanding of primary narcissism as primordially relational (in Heidegger's sense), which indicates time as the organizing principle of psychic structure, as well as of libidinal structures generally;
- Winnicott's crucial notion of potential, transitional space-time, and his understanding of how and of what it means that this can manifest itself "spiritually" at the level of material objects;
- Bollas's project of rehabilitating Freud's methods of free association and freely-floating attention—the Freudian pair, which points us beyond the figure of the classical, intersubjective dyad—and the non-metaphysical understanding of mind they imply;
- Stiegler's genealogy of technics, which demands a rethinking not only of the concept of the superego, but of the analytic frame as the most radical intersection of psychoanalysis and politics today;
- Nietzsche's critique of nihilism, and his understanding of individuation as a means of combatting nihilism, as providing a new way of thinking interpretation as the basis for a clinical, therapeutic practice.

Notes

1 Laplanche (1989) writes,

> Any epistemology or theory of psychoanalysis must take account of the very basic fact that the human subject is a theorizing being and a being which theorizes itself, by which I mean that it is a self-theorizing being or, should the term 'theorize' seem too intimidating, a self-symbolizing being. (p. 10)

> For Aristotle, this self-symbolizing is what makes real thinking an articulation of desire, as the dynamic capacity to be *moved* by the world, and as that which links the human to the divine, the latter conceived by Aristotle (not unlike Freud's unconscious, at least where Freud's method is concerned) as thought-thinking-itself (Aristotle 1998, pp. 373–375). "Theory," it should be remembered, derives from the Greek *theoria* (contemplation), which comes from *Theos* (God).

2 In a similar vein, Raoul Vaneigem writes, "Enhanced by human consciousness, life is a weapon that creates instead of killing. It is the source of a lesson that in these troubled times needs to be heard: what must be contested is the totalitarian system which oppresses

126   *Weapons*

us and not the people who believe they are in charge of it when in fact they are no more than its pale avatars … But our war cannot be limited to browsing amid the ruins of market civilization. On the contrary, it must prepare, beyond all war, to create new conditions for life. That is the only way to break the grip of the commodity once and for all" (2019, pp. 70–71).

3 "Club 27" is a pop cultural term referencing the common age at which a number of musicians associated with the counterculture (Brian Jones, Jimi Hendrix, Janis Joplin, Amy Winehouse, etc.) died, typically by accidental drug overdose. This term had already emerged as a signifier of cultural authenticity by the time Kurt Cobain made the cynical decision to "join the club."

4 Other relevant titles by authors associating themselves with speculative realism include, but are not limited to: Brassier (2007), Thacker (2010, 2011), Trigg (2014) and Peak (2014). Though not formally associated with this movement, Ligotti (2010) occupies a central place here.

5 Winnicott is worth rehearsing here with respect to intensity as an aspect of transitional space: "This intermediate area of experience, unchallenged in respect of its belonging to inner or external (shared) reality, constitutes the greater part of the infant's experience, and is throughout life retained in the *intense experiencing* that belongs to the arts and to religion and to imaginative living, and to creative scientific work" (1970, p. 14; emphasis added). Though he does not say so explicitly, it is difficult to imagine Winnicott not including the clinical practice of psychoanalysis as belonging to the category of "creative scientific work."

6 Deleuze: "I think subjectification, events, and brains are more or less the same thing. What we most lack is a belief in the world, it's been taken from us. If you believe in the world you precipitate events, however inconspicuous, that elude control, you engender new space-times, however small their surface or volume" (1995, p. 176).

References

Aristotle (1998). *The Metaphysics*. Trans. H. Lawson-Tancred. New York: Penguin Books.

Berardi, F. (2015). *Heroes: Mass Murder and Suicide*. New York: Verso.

Bollas, C. (2018). *Meaning and Melancholia: Life in the Age of Bewilderment*. New York: Routledge.

Brassier, R. (2007). *Nihil Unbound: Enlightenment and Extinction*. New York: Palgrave Macmillan.

Crary, J. (2013). *24/7*. New York: Verso.

Deleuze, G. (1983). *Nietzsche and Philosophy*. Trans. H. Tomlinson. New York: Columbia University Press.

Deleuze, G. (1994). *Difference and Repetition*. Trans. P. Patton. New York: Columbia University Press.

Deleuze, G. (1995). *Negotiations*. Trans. M. Joughin. New York: Columbia University Press.

Derrida, J. (1976). *Of Grammatology*. Trans. G. Spivak. Baltimore, MD: Johns Hopkins University Press.

Derrida, J. (1978). *Dissemination*. Trans. B. Johnson. Chicago, IL: University of Chicago Press.

devi dasi, J.(2016). *Venom and Honey*. Martinet Press.

Fincher, D. (dir.). (1999). *Fight Club*.

Freud, S. (1927). *The Future of an Illusion*. S.E. XXI, pp. 1–56.

Freud, S. (1930). *Civilization and Its Discontents*. S.E. XXI, pp. 57–146.

Weapons 127

Heidegger, M. (1969). *Discourse on Thinking*. Trans. J.H. Anderson and E.H. Freund. New York: Harper Torchbooks.

Heidegger, M. (1995). *The Fundamental Concepts of Metaphysics: World, Finitude, Solitude*. Trans. W. McNeill and N. Walker. Bloomington, IN: Indiana University Press.

Horkheimer, M. and Adorno, T. (2007). *Dialectic of Enlightenment*. Trans. E. Jephcott. Stanford, CA: Stanford University Press.

Kierkegaard, S. (1962). *The Present Age: On the Death of Rebellion*. Trans. A. Dru. New York: Harper Collins.

Kirk, G.S., Raven, J.E. and Schofield, M. (Eds.). (1983). *The Presocratic Philosophers*, Second Edition. Cambridge University Press.

Laplanche, J. (1989). *New Foundations for Psychoanalysis*. Trans. D. Macey. Cambridge, MA: Basil Blackwell.

Ligotti, T. (2010). *The Conspiracy Against the Human Race*. New York: Hippocampus Press.

Marcuse, H. (1965). *One-Dimensional Man: Studies in the Ideology of Advanced Industrial Society*. New York: Beacon Press.

Mason, J. (1992). *Siege*. Denver, CO: Storm Books.

Meillasoux, Q. (2009). *After Finitude: An Essay on the Necessity of Contingency*. Trans. R. Brassier. New York: Bloomsbury Academic.

Nietzsche, F. (1967). *On the Genealogy of Morals* and *Ecco Homo*. Ed. and Trans. W. Kaufman. New York: Vintage Books.

Nietzsche, F. (1968). *The Will to Power*. Ed. and Trans. W. Kaufman. New York: Vintage Books.

Nietzsche, F. (1996). *Human, All Too Human: A Book for Free Spirits*. Trans. R.J. Hollingdale. Cambridge University Press.

Nietzsche, N. (2001). *The Gay Science*. Trans. J. Nauckhoff and A. del Caro. Cambridge University Press.

Nietzsche, F. (2005). *The Anti-Christ, Ecco Homo, Twilight of the Idols*. Trans. J. Norman. Cambridge University Press.

Nolan, C. (dir.). (2012). *Batman: The Dark Knight Rises*.

Palahniuk, C. (1996). *Fight Club*. New York: Owl Books.

Peak, D. (2014). *The Spectacle of the Void*. Schism Press.

Plotnitsky, A. (2002). *The Knowable and the Unknowable: Modern Science, Nonclassical Thought, and the "Two Cultures."* Ann Arbor, MI: University of Michigan Press.

Sloterdijk, P. (2012). *The Art of Philosophy: Wisdom as a Practice*. Trans. K. Margolis. New York: Columbia University Press.

Stiegler, B. (1998). *Technics and Time, 1: The Fault of Epimetheus*. Trans. R. Beardsworth and G. Collins. Stanford, CA: Stanford University Press.

Stiegler, B. (2011). *The Decadence of Industrial Democracies*. Trans. D. Ross and S. Arnold. New York: Polity.

Stiegler, B. (2014a). *Symbolic Misery: Vol. 1: The Hyperindustrial Epoch*. Trans. B. Norman. New York: Polity.

Stiegler, B. (2014b). *The Lost Spirit of Capitalism*. Trans. D. Ross. New York: Polity.

Stiegler, B. (2015). *Symbolic Misery, Volume 2: The Katastrophē of the Sensible*. Trans. B. Norman. New York: Polity Press.

Stiegler, B. (2020). "Covid 19: Insight from the Angle of Memory." Trans. D. Ross. https://www.academia.edu/42827840/

Tempel ov Blood (2014). *Iron Gates*. Martinet Press.

Thacker, E. (2010). *After Life*. Chicago, IL: University of Chicago Press.

128 *Weapons*

Thacker, E. (2011). *In the Dust of This Planet: Horror of Philosophy Vol. 1*. Washington, DC: Zero Books.

Trigg, D. (2014). *The Thing: A Phenomenology of Horror*. Washington, DC: Zero Books.

Vaneigem, R. (2019). *A Letter to My Children and the Children of the World to Come*. Trans. D. Nicholson-Smith. Oakland, CA: PM Press.

Vitale, F. (2018). *Biodeconstruction: Jacques Derrida and the Life Sciences*. Trans. M. Senatore. New York: SUNY Press.

Weber, M. (2012). *The Protestant Ethic and the Spirit of Capitalism: and Other Writings*. New York: Penguin.

Winnicott, D.W. (1970). *Playing and Reality*. New York: Routledge.

Index

abstraction 8n1, 36, 40, 101, 109
adaptation 111, 124
addiction 2, 68, 110, 124
adequatio see correspondence
Adler, A. 17
adolescence 6, 30, 79, 97, 116–17
Adorno, T. 58n2, 109
aesthetic 58n2, 61, 72, 88, 102, 121; of
  being 66; of care 66; dimension 90;
  experience 60, 62; frame 65; maternal
  62–3; moment 61–4, 73, 75, 98n1;
  see also Bollas, C.
affect 21, 45, 61–2, 66, 69, 75, 102, 111–12
affirmation 102, 104, 107–8
agency 5, 13, 29–31, 47, 49, 107
aggression 108
aidos see shame
aisthēsis 61–4, 69
alethea see unconcealment
anaclitic 20, 28
analysand 70–4, 75
analytic ecology 72
Andreas-Salomé, L. 18
Angst see anxiety
Anlehnung see leaning
annihilation 105, 107
Anthropocene 93, 121
anthropology 53
Antigone 6, 79–80, 85–8, 90–2, 93–8, 118;
  Creon 95–7, 80, 85–7, 90, 92; Ismene
  92; Polynices 85, 91, 96; Tiresias 87
anxiety 18, 45–6, 74, 81, 124
apathy 106
Aporia 88
apparitional 63, 65, 72–4
Aristotelian rationalism 4
as-structure 42, 44–5, 69, 82–4, 98
atē 81, 88–91
Atomwaffen 120–1

attention 15, 62, 80; freely floating 70,
  76n6, 125; hovering 69, 76n5, 100;
  economy 6, 112
auseinander zu legen 82
Ausgelegt 82
authenticity 50, 58n2, 80, 126n3;
  see also Eigentlich
authority 35–7, 86, 92, 95, 97, 120
autonomy 26, 47, 79, 117
autopoiesis 6, 75, 106, 125
autos see self-giving
Auvinen, P. 119

Barratt, B. 76n4
Batman: The Dark Knight Rises 119–20
beauty 88, 90
Berardi, F. 117–9
biological determinism 10
Bion, W. 76n3, 76n6
bio-power 113
Birksted-Breen, D. 76n6
Blake, J. 103
Bollas, C. 5–7, 28, 58n1, 60–75, 76n3–4,
  76n6, 98n1, 113–4, 118, 123–5; "The
  Aesthetic Moment and the Search for
  Transformation" 60, 66; "The
  Transformational Object" 60, 64, 66
boredom 123–4
Bowie, D. 117
Brassier, R. 126n4
Brooks, R. 103
Burroughs, W. 108, 123

calculation 115
care: aesthetics 66; *Antigone* 85;
  environmental 63, 65–6; caregiving 3,
  22, 24, 27, 29, 57, 61, 63–5, 68, 75, 101,
  114, 122; caretaking 62–5, 68; child- 35;
  future 48; investment 5, 25, 31; libido 28;

130   *Index*

maternal 58n1, 62, 64–7, 71; other- 19, 28; parental 28, 57; self 13, 19, 24, 28–9, 106; unconcealment 44
Cartesian 41, 43
catatonia 117
cathexis 5, 15, 19, 23–4, 27, 52
censorship 70, 113, 124
Cesare, M. 32n2
Charcot, J. 2
Chasseguet-Smirgel, J. 33n6
Cho, S. 119
choral ode 80–1, 85–6, 88–9
Christianity 54, 90–1
citizenship 94–5
civilization 21, 54, 93–4, 107–8, 111, 113, 115, 117, 126n2
clinic 3, 5, 7, 57, 76n6, 101, 115; approach 3; environment 50, 55; experience 2, 60; frame 70, 124; Heidegger 88; interpretation 2–3, 7, 56–7, 66, 125; intervention 6; Lacan 94–5; method 69; patient 22; practice 1, 3–4, 6, 60, 125, 126n5; procedures 3; psychoanalytic 2, 32, 58, 100, 123–4; reverie 76n3; session 70; work 7
Club 27, 115, 126n3
Cobain, K. 117, 126n3
coercion 107
cogito see Descartes
cognition 15, 44, 61, 63
cognitive 3, 5, 45, 64, 67–8, 98n1; coherence 61; function 62, 69; memory 62; paradigm 61; pre- 61; recall 63; sciences 109
Columbine 116–20
communication 70, 72–4, 111
community 4, 17, 30, 85, 92, 95–7
composition 95, 109
computer science 109
conceptual creation 105
concreteness 3, 8n1, 76, 96, 106, 114, 120
confinement 101
connection 13, 54–6, 60, 83, 100, 120–1
consciousness 14–5, 18, 44, 62, 73, 109, 111–3, 125n2; conscious choice 10; conscious representation 51; conscious retrieval 62; conscious subject 63; conscious thought 45; violence 117
consistencies 93, 97
consumerism 32, 37, 68, 123; consumer 2–3, 109–10
contemplation 125n1
contribution 115

control 4, 20, 24, 58, 94, 115, 120, 122–3, 126n6; of consciousness 113; of desire 32; extreme 7; frameworks of 124; logics of 124; obtain 24; societies 108, 113; of symbols 112; techniques of 108
conversion 18, 25
correspondence 18, 42, 56
COVID-19 101, 104
creativity 6–7, 17, 65, 68–9, 71, 73–5, 105, 111, 122, 124; creative 9, 18, 48, 85, 108, 117; creative act 31–2; creative constitution 16; creative process 33n6; creative scientific work 126n5
culture 2–5, 21, 27, 41, 50, 88, 105, 109, 111; anti- 116; civilized 117; commercial 117; contemporary 101, 111; counterculture 126n3; cultural aesthetics 58n2; cultural asset 107; cultural authenticity 126n3; cultural conditions 3; cultural contributors 108; cultural development 54; cultural field 30; cultural ideals 25; cultural injunction 115; cultural institutions 102; cultural production 7, 75, 93; cultural recognition 6; cultural shift 36; cultural sphere 25; cultural studies 1; cultural terms 92; cultural trend 36; cultural vacuum 116; culturally valued 22, 30; industrialized 111; industries 109, 112, 115; popular 116; postmodern 36, 68; pure 5, 23, 96; sociocultural 2, 4, 31; retro 115

Da-sein: analysis of 81; being 39–40, 44–6, 58n2, 72; Dasein 123; death 89; disclosure 44–5, 50, 53, 90, 125; essence of 43; essential trait 98; freedom of 105; historical 85; as itself 50; as mine 43–4; *Mitda-Sein* 44; as object 43; occurrence 40; ontological 49, 58, 75; openness 69, 125; phenomenological analysis 65; structure of 57, 82–4; as subject 43; thrownness 57; in tragedy 80; violence 82, 86, 93; and the world 41, 86, 125
das Ding 91–2
das Man 81
death: *Antigone* (chorus) 83, 87, 89; being-toward- 83; Bollas 113; COVID-19 104; "Death and Fire" 35; drive 17, 52; Heidegger 83; history 30; instinct 5, 23, 52, 54, 96; Lacan 86–7; limit beyond all limits 83–4; limit of 93, 97–8; machine 121; of the mind 7; potential 7; of rebellion 105–6; second death 87–8;

Index 131

"Septet of Death" 35; between two 7, 88, 92; uncanny thing 84
deconstruction 65, 79, 93, 97–8, 109
defense 4, 52, 55
defiance 85–6, 90, 92–5, 97
deinon 81–2, 84, 86, 88, 94
deinotaton 80
Deleuze, G. 101, 108, 122–3, 126n6
deliberation 106
depression 23, 101, 109, 117
deprivation 110, 118
Derrida, J. 65–6, 74–5, 75n176n3, 93, 95–8, 109–10, 112, 114, 123–4
Descartes, R. 43, 45, 63
desexualizaiton 22, 25, 111; *see also* libido
desire 3, 5, 14, 21; *Antigone* 86, 88, 96; Aristotle 125n1; autonomy 26; collective 100; collapse of 109; constitution of 95, 98; consumerism 110; control of 32; cultivation of 102, 106–7; drive and 32n2; drives become 23, 25, 31–2, 16–7, 21; emergence of 28, 67; *Fight Club* 116; fight for 114; generation of 108; and historical time 28; individual 3, 94–5, 100; internalizing transformation of 57; *Iron Gates* 121; Lacan 91; object of 15, 67, 91–2, 97; parental objects 96; portrayal of 116; regression from 95; thinking 15; unconscious 64
destruction 3–4, 6, 23, 101, 103, 107–8, 110, 122; self- 102, 115–6, 123
Destruktion 41
desublimation 100
desymbolization 8n1, 100, 106, 114
development 1, 4–6, 27, 107; becoming 29; child 24; cultural 54; of the ego 22; experience 60; figure of the father 27; grammatization 112; history 58; individual 26, 66, 102; of intermediary forms 103; levels of 32; of the libido 19; memory of 64; Oedipal 33n6; past 75; post-adolescence 116; potential 26; primary narcissism 46, 49; primitive 46; process of 14, 29, 97–8, 109; psychic structures 57; psychoanalysis qua 52–3, 59; psychological 111; self- 29; socialized 29; solitude 100
diachronization 114
dialogue 5, 7, 58, 62–3, 76n6, 80, 91
différance 95, 97
differentiation 19–20, 23–6, 29–31, 45–8, 55–7, 106; undifferentiated 52
digitalization 94

dikē 84–7, 90, 93, 95, 97; *see also* justice
Dionysian 116
discharge 52
disclosure: beings disclose themselves 83–4, 97; being in the world 124; Bollas 74; Da-sein 44–5, 82, 90, 125; disclose and openness 50; discloses life 107; disclosing something as something 56; interpretive 50, 53–5, 57, 85, 125; of others 44; phenomenological 69; play of pain 88; of possibility 43, 50, 69; primary narcissism 74; self- 74; tragedy 85; unconcealment 44; unconscious suffering 123; understanding discloses 40; violence 83, 97
disruption 54, 56, 111–2
divine 53–4, 96, 125n1
domesticity 106, 109
dream 14–5, 21, 28; become real 16, 26; capacity to 16, 32; daydreams 16; dreamer 32; drive and 12; faculty of dreaming 21; form of thinking 14–6, 62; function of 14; hallucination 15; phenomena 15; repressed 112; solitude 100; wish fulfilment 16; violence 104, 118; world of the 16
drive: *Antigone* 92, 96; -based enjoyment 21; desire 21, 25, 31–2, 32n2, 57, 91, 95–6; classical drive theorist 38; concept of 10–4, 16, 57; constitution of 13; control over 24; death 17, 52; deconstruction 97; dimension of 10; dream 12; economizing 15–6, 24, 98, 108; ego 19, 112; emergence of 28; explosion of 113; fantasy 14; Freudian 10, 51; gratification 17, 28, 57, 103; id 15, 24; of the individual 113; instinct 9–10–1 13, 32n2; libidinal energy of 26, 52; libidinal vicissitudes 31; life 51; Nietzsche 52; object 10–1, 13, 24, 27; pleasure 52; primacy of 53; reduction of 26; sexual 19; sublimation 10, 21–3, 26, 92–3, 95, 122; *Trieb* 91; unconscious 10; violence doing 81, 86
dualism 11, 13
dyad 70–1, 125

echo 74
education 101–2
ego: formation 22, 74; ideal 5, 20–3, 26–31, 33n6, 47, 75, 96, 98, 118; organization 48, 76n2; primitive 26
Eigentlich 58n2, 50, 89; *see also* authenticity

132 Index

empathy 109, 114, 117, 124
emptiness 39, 54, 105, 120, 123–4
endosomatic 11
Enlightenment 4, 36
environment 1–2, 4–5, 7; absence of 40;
  care 29, 63–6, 68; clinical 50, 55;
  contemporary 2; determined 94;
  developmental 6, 14; environmental
  conditions 3; environmental demand 52,
  111; exploitative 123; external 66, 68; as
  historicity 50; hostility 109; integrated
  with 46; interactions with 32; maternal
  62, 64, 67; mind 13, 71–2, 74; at one
  with one's 49; post-modern 94; relational
  66; self and 4, 22, 41, 54–5, 62; shared
  25; social and political 1; surrounding 41;
  technology saturated 95; time 49; total
  66–7, 71
enviro-somatic 67–8, 75, 114
envy see ressentiment
eo ipso 108
epistemology 61, 125n1
eristic 114
Eros 17, 51–3, 97, 106
erotic 12, 24–6, 56–7; auto-eroticism
  13, 26
essence: of being 61; of Da-sein 43; drive as
  16; human 84, 90, 98n2; nihilism 6; of
  psychical processes 62; of the pursuit of
  justice 95; of sublimation 21, 26, 97; of
  thought as reason 15; of tragedy 86, 91;
  undecidability 110; as whatness 43
ethics 91–2, 94
evolution 1, 9, 65, 93–5, 97, 108, 110, 115,
  117; de-evolution 117
existential 6, 46, 53, 61, 65, 67–9, 75;
  known 64; interpretation 86; memory
  62–4, 98n1; mood 109; recollection 62;
  self 43; space-time 63–4
experimentation 104; experiment in
  thinking 47; live experimentally 105
external: coercion 107; environment 66,
  68; externalization 97; gratification 66;
  mind 12; objects 27, 41, 48; opposition
  84; position 29; primary narcissism 46;
  reality 126; world 1, 16, 30–1, 32n3,
  47, 122

falsity 42
fantasy 13–4, 16, 19, 21–2, 28, 56, 69, 115,
  119–21
feeding 12–3, 62
fetish 110

fiction 104–6, 115, 121
Fight Club; see also Palahniuk, C.
fighting 113, 116
financialization 3, 6, 105
Fincher, D. 116
fixation 47
Fliess 14
Floyd, G. 103
forgetting 38, 41–3, 55
Foucault, M. 106, 108, 113
frame: aesthetic 65; analytic 71–3, 123, 125;
  clinical 70, 124; framework 1, 10, 13, 19,
  24, 38, 41, 43, 46, 51–3, 63, 67, 69, 93,
  124; of mind 71–3; neutral 75;
  psychoanalytic 75; as-relation 72, 74;
  technical 67, 72
free association 69–71, 76n4, 100, 125
Freud, A. 76n5
Freud, S.: Beyond the Pleasure Principle 52;
  Civilization and Its Discontents 16, 23, 113,
  122; das Unbehagen 123; Ego and the Id 16,
  20, 22–3, 30; Fundamental Concepts of
  Metaphysics: World, Finitude, Solitude 122;
  Group Psychology and the Analysis of the
  Ego 20, 23; Interpretation of Dreams 14–5,
  18; "Mourning and Melancholia" 20–3;
  "On Narcissism" 18, 20, 27, 33n4; An
  Outline of Psycho-Analysis 10, 16;
  Preliminaries to a Metapsychology 17; Three
  Essays on the Theory of Sexuality 10, 12,
  14–5, 21; "Two Principles of the Mental
  Functioning" 13
Fug 84
fundamentalism 96–7, 114

gefügt 98n2
Geheimnis 123
Gemes, K. 9
generational difference 28, 58
gerontocracy 94
Geworfenheit see thrownness
Gödel, K. 110
Goethe 12, 102
good 21, 23–4, 86, 91–2, 95–6, 106, 116
grammar of being 28, 65, 114
grammatization 66, 73, 112–3
gratification 8n1, 17, 21, 25–6, 28, 57, 66,
  103, 122
Great War 113
Greenberg, J. 76n5
grief 111

hallucination 14–5

Index   133

Hamlet 87
Harris, E. *see* Columbine
Hegel 37, 54, 87, 91
Heidegger, M.: *Being and Time* 5, 38, 42–5, 53, 81–3; *Hölderlin's Hymn "The Ister"* 79–80, 86; *Introduction to Metaphysics* 80–1, 83, 87; "On Time and Being" 35; *What Is Called Thinking?* 37
Heimlichkeit 123
Heisenberg, W. 36, 51
Heraclitus 4, 107
hero 117, 121
Heroes: Mass Murder and Suicide see Berardi, F.
historical philosophizing 104
historical time 28
historicity 40–1, 49–50, 54, 57, 65, 83, 96
Holmes, J. 119–21
homicide 104
homosexuality 10
Horkheimer, M. 109
hostility 109, 113, 115
humanism 4, 110; *see also* Western Secular Enlightenment
humanity 43, 53, 83, 124; *see also* inhumanity
hunger 10, 13
hybridity 7
hypokeimenon 45
hysteria 2, 18

id 10–1, 15, 24–6, 30–1, 47–9, 70, 76n2, 76n5
idealization 21–3, 26, 28–30, 75, 96, 103, 115
identification 23, 58, 113; appeal to the id by means of 25; concept of 21; ego differentiates itself 25; idealizing 75; object-cathexis 24; with the other 24; parental objects 96; Plato 91; with primary 3, 27–9, 109, 112; processes of 27–8; projective 68; proto-perceptual 67–8; secondary 27–8; sublimation 26, 30; unconscious 111
ideology 4, 7, 103, 120
idioumai 64
illness 2, 83, 89, 101–2, 104, 107
imagination 5, 73; imaginary 91
immiseration 109
impulse 10, 30–1, 122
individuation: autopoiesis 75, 106; collective 112; combatting nihilism 125; Da-sein 46, 58, 90; differential repetition

88; disindividuation 109; to individuate 20–1, 32, 46, 48, 92; individuated singularity 32; interiority 112; opposite of 45; process of 4, 26, 29, 64, 79, 109; psyche 112; radical 43, 50, 55–6, 71, 74–5, 90, 124; spiritual 98; sublimating 97; technical 94–6
industrialization 94, 111–2, 121
in-fans 15, 62
infant 12–6, 19, 27–8, 32, 46, 57, 58n1, 62–7, 71–2, 126n5
InfoMatin 101
in-formation 74, 106, 111, 124
inheritance 1, 9, 30, 48, 58n1, 61, 65, 69, 76n2, 95, 97, 111–2, 117–8
inhumanity 114, 124; *see also* humanity
instinct 10–1, 13, 17, 26, 92, 103, 107, 111, 122; biological 10–4, 16, 26–8; death 5, 23, 52, 54, 96; drive 9, 11, 32n2; ego 19–20; experience 12; idealization of 21; infant 67; *Instinkt* 92; overlordship of 103; perverse 122; sexual 19–20; *Triebe* 11, 19, 32n1, 58n2; unconscious 51
integration 2, 13, 19, 50, 54, 67
intensity 15, 122, 126n5
interdetermination 3
intergenerational 4, 30, 93, 101, 119
internalization 12, 24, 29, 48, 57–8, 74, 104, 107, 124
interpretation 43–4, 50, 55, 74, 82, 98, 104–6; *Antigone* 85–6; *Ausgelegte* 82; of being 39; clinic of 2–3, 125, 56; Da-sein 40, 83; psychoanalytic act of 54, 57; therapeutic 3, 125; of time 41
interpsychic 57; *see also* intrapsychic
intersubjectivity 25, 70, 72; *see also* subjectivity
intrapsychic 57, 111; *see also* interpsychic
invention 50
inversion *see* homosexuality
investment 5, 19–20, 24–6, 28, 31
Iron Gates 115, 120–1
isolation 41, 43, 71; *see also* solitude

Jones, E. 17–8
Joseph, B. 76n6
Jouissance 95
Jung, C. 17
justice 84–6, 93, 95–7, 98n1, 110; *see also* dike

Kant, E. 41, 51, 58, 63, 88, 90–1, 121
Kaplan, D. 9

134 *Index*

Kierkegaard 105–7, 108, 116, 123
Klebold, D. *see* Columbine
Klee, P. 35
knowing 44, 67, 84–6, 88, 111, 123; *see also techne*
knowledge 1–2, 5, 35–7, 61, 85, 88, 93, 95, 105, 109–11; technical 35–7; transmission of
krinein 94

Lacan, J. 5–7, 23, 32n2, 51, 69, 87–98, 98n3
language 14–5, 28, 62–3, 65, 82, 87, 90, 98n2
LaPlanche, J. 10, 12, 18, 125n1
l'a-venir see to-come
law 26, 29, 79, 85, 87, 95–8, 104–5, 108; *see also nomos*
leaning 12
l'etant 87
l'etre 87
Levi-Strauss 88
libido 19–20, 52, 75, 122; cathexis 19; desexualization of 22, 25; development of the 19; displacement of 22; ego-19; libidinal complement 19; libidinal economy 15, 19, 25, 53, 56, 111, 113, 115, 125; libidinal effort 19; libidinal energy 26, 52; libidinal investment 15, 24, 28, 31; libidinal relation 23, 56; libidinal structures 125; object- 19–20, 24–5, 29, 31, 56–7; narcissistic 24–5, 29, 31, 56–7; self-care 19; theory 19, 52–3; vicissitudes 30–1
Ligotti, T. 126n4
linguistics 65, 90, 109, 112–3
linkage 54–5
Loewald, H.: "Ego and Reality" 53; "The Experience of Time" 49; *Sublimation* 5, 50; "Superego and Time" 46, 53
logic 2, 20, 25, 31, 41, 64–6, 74, 97, 98n1, 110, 121
logos 42; *see also* phenomenology

Macquarrie, J. 58n2
Mahler, M. 13
mania 104, 115
manifest 42–3, 81, 85, 124–5; manifestation 19, 82, 84, 109, 117
Manson, C. 120
Marcuse, H. 57, 108
marketplace 2–4, 32, 68, 95–6, 105, 119, 124

martyr 91, 117
Marx, K. 110
Mason, J. *see Siege*
material 53–6, 70, 73, 84, 111; inscription 93, 109; quasi- 73; objects 125; practice 102; reality 51
materialism 51; materialist 79, 93, 97–8, 93, 102
maternal 58, 62–7, 71
mathematics 110
meaningfulness 39–40
meaninglessness 103, 120
megalomania 32n3
Meillasoux, Q. 121
memorialization 55
memory 14–5, 47–8, 61, 101, 112, 114; Antigone 97; capacity for 13; cognitive 61–2; existential 61–4, 68–9, 75, 98n1; experience of 62; form of 14–5, 17, 62; intergenerational 119; memorization 14, 63, 93; microdynamics of 33n6, 49; sexuality 13, 17; as repetition 28, 65; retrieval 14, 68
mental health 1, 3, 53
metaphysics 38, 40–3, 45, 52–4, 58n1, 60, 63–4, 66, 69, 72, 98n1, 101, 103, 105, 110, 121, 125
metapsychology 16, 57
millennials 111–2
Milner, M. 61
modernity 50, 103
moment: aesthetic 60–4, 66, 73, 75, 98n1; *see also* aesthetic experience; sublime
moral 5, 23, 30, 49, 84, 103, 105, 107; civilized morality 30; moralizing 91
mystery 123–4

Näcke, P. 19
narcissism 19–21, 56, 96, 110; "On Narcissism" 18, 20, 27, 33n4; primary 19, 22–3, 27–8, 46, 49, 52, 54–5, 57, 63, 74–5, 118, 125
Neo-Nazi 120
Nettleton, S. 60
neurosis 16, 18–9, 32n3
neutrality 71, 75, 76n5
Nietzsche, F. 6–7, 12, 58, 100–8, 115, 123–5
nihilism 6, 10–7, 109, 114–5, 118, 125
nomos 26, 79; *see also* law
normativity 84

object: fixed 10; maternal 62, 67; parental

Index 135

96; relations 11, 13–4, 24, 29, 38, 44–5, 56–7, 68, 71; transitional 31, 61, 110
objective presence 43–6, 63, 68–9, 72, 84, 120, 123
Oedipus complex 24, 29–31, 33n6
ontogenetic 57, 64
ontology 40, 42–6, 49, 57–8, 58n1, 60, 63–6, 74–5, 79, 86, 93, 98, 105, 123
openness 12, 26, 28, 43–6, 48, 50, 69, 71, 74, 105, 125
oppression 2, 108, 112–3, 123–4
Order of Nine Angles 120–1
organic 2, 110, 112

Palahniuk, C. 116, 119–20; see also Fight Club
Pan 119
panic 81, 104, 118–9
Parmenides 63, 80, 85
participation 109–10, 115
passion 53, 57, 84–6, 98n2, 106
Peak, D. 126n4
perception 61–2, 69, 112–3, 118
perversion 10, 19, 21, 33n6
phainesthai see phenomenology
pharmakon 110
phenomenology 42
phenomenon see phenomenology
philosophy 35–7, 41, 80, 85, 101, 124
phos see phenomenology
phusis 81, 84, 86
phylogenetic 57
Plato 54, 63, 91–2, 95, 110; Platonic idealism 4
play-space 63, 65, 75
pleasure 12–4, 17, 22, 25, 51–3, 117, 122; principle 17, 20, 26, 52
polemos 112; polemical 114
polis 82, 84
political 1, 3–4, 6–7, 18, 79, 84, 94–5, 100–1, 110, 112, 114–7, 120–1, 125
Pontalis 18
populism 114
poros 81–3, 88
positivism 114
positivity 108
postmodernism 36, 68, 103, 120
primary repetition 26
printing 65
projection 18, 21, 27–9, 68, 80, 83–4, 90, 96–7; poetic
proletarianization 110
psyche 24, 26, 29–30, 35, 47, 57; child's 23;

differentiated 48; Freudian 58; infantile 27; inner 55; organized 54, 56; structuralization of 75; subjective 27
psychecology 71
psychic: apparatus 11, 65; differentiation 26; future 49; life 111; past 48–9; reality 51; structure 15, 24–6, 30, 46–8, 49, 52–4, 56–7, 63, 65, 111, 114, 125
psychopathology 68
psychosis 19, 32n3, 45, 102
publicity 105
Putnam, J.J 18

quarantine see COVID-19
quiet 71–4, 123; see also silence

racism 104
reality 11, 15–6, 19–20, 30, 32n3, 51–3, 55, 63, 75, 76n3, 94–5, 117, 119–21, 126n5
reality testing 15
rebellion 105–7
reductionism 1, 11
reflection 17, 20, 36, 43–4, 47, 57, 70, 80, 87, 90, 101, 106, 114
regression 1, 23, 47, 95–6, 98, 124
Reis, B. 71
relationality 20, 38, 42, 44–5, 67, 70, 95
relativism 36, 103
religion 106, 126n5
representation 11, 42, 50–1, 54, 58n2, 62, 67, 106; representational cognition 61; representational knowing 67; representational thinking 70
repression 2, 8n1, 22, 24, 52, 55–6, 92, 113
Republican National Convention 104
res cogitans 45
res extensa 45
resistance 3–4, 7, 102, 105, 108, 110, 121, 124
resourcefulness 88–9
responsibility 4, 6, 28, 94–5, 103–5
ressentiment 102, 107, 123
revenge 102, 111
Robinson, E. 58n2

Sachevorstellungen see thing presentations
Sade 87–8, 91
satire 106, 116
Schofield 107
Schreber 18
second death 87–8
Sein see being
separation 54–5, 72, 83, 120

136   *Index*

sexual difference 27–8
sexual function 53
sexuality 6, 10, 12–5, 17, 53–4
shame 48, 93, 95
sickness 89, 93, 106–7
Siege 120
silence 62, 71, 123; *see also* quiet
Simondon 95
simulacrum 108, 120
Sloterdijk, P. 100–1
snowflake 116
social networking 112, 124
social values 91–2, 97
socio-cultural 2, 4, 31
solitude *see* isolation
Sophocles 6, 79
Sorge see care
soul 2, 13, 45, 87, 108
space: becoming- 61–3, 66–7, 119–20;
   between 4, 11; as extension 45; internal
   114; intersubjective recognition 71;
   object relations 38, 44; potential 74, 108;
   psychoanalytic 74–5; relational 72–4;
   solitary 101; and time 63–4, 100, 123–5,
   126n6, 66; transitional 100–1
spatial 29, 50, 54; anteriority 42; model 27;
   relation 47; spatialization 29
spectral 96–7
Spenglerian 103
Spielberg, S. 118
Spielraum see play-space
spiritual experience 54
Stiegler, B. 6–7, 58, 79, 93–8, 100–1,
   108–15, 123–5
stimulus 11
Strachey, J. 17–8, 32n1–2, 58n2
stupidity 108
subjecticide 112
subjectivity 24, 41, 43–4, 52, 74, 88, 117;
   subjective experience 30, 65; subjective
   interiority 29, 45, 73; subjective meaning
   72, 83; subjective psyche 27; subjective
   self 25, 68; subjective truth 55;
   see also intersubjectivity
subjugation 82–3
sublime 31, 54, 88, 90–2, 94, 96–7, 114,
   118–9, 122
subsistence 110
suffering 2–4, 6, 87–8, 112, 122–3
suicide 23, 101, 106–7, 112, 115, 117–8
sum see Descartes
supra-individual organism 114
survival 62, 100, 110

symbol 54–6, 65, 105, 108–9, 112, 123;
   deymbolization 8n1, 100, 106, 114;
   symbolic 4, 54–5, 57, 58n2, 74–5, 91, 93,
   109–10, 112, 114–16, 120, 123;
   symbolism 55; symbolization 3, 8n1,
   54–5, 71, 106, 109, 122–3, 124;
   symbolize 3, 27, 58, 100, 109–10, 119,
   125n1
synchronization 114
synthesis 37, 42, 45

Tarantino, Q. 118
technē 84–6, 90; *see also* knowing
technics 65, 124
technology 1, 3, 72, 84, 93–5, 110–1;
   digital
telepathy 74
Tempel ov Blood 120
temporality 40, 47, 49–50, 54, 57, 123;
   aesthetic 60, 62–3; ecstatic 45, 57, 82;
   element 76n6; erotic 57; horizon 48;
   implication 39; modes 48; ontology 60;
   organization 48, 54, 56; originary 40;
   precedence 42; primitive dimension 75;
   printing 75 54; psychic structures 47;
   relatedness 40–2, 49; temporalization 29,
   69; transformational 68
tertiary retention 97
Thacker, E. 126n4
thematic 54, 65, 91, 108–9
theoretical biology 109
theoria 125n1
Theos 125n1
thing-presentations 4
thoughtfulness 71, 112
thrownness 57
Thunberg, G. 93
total administration 108
totalitarianism 102, 110, 125n2
tradition 4, 9, 15, 30, 36, 41, 45, 50, 54, 85,
   90, 95–8, 103, 124
tragedy 80, 85–6, 91–2, 97
Trakl, G. 35
transduction 95
transference 18, 53, 94, 96
transformation 2–4, 12, 24, 27, 31, 33n4,
   36, 47, 61–4, 67, 69, 72–3, 102–3,
   106–7, 110, 115, 123; "The Aesthetic
   Moment and the Search for
   Transformation" 60, 66; *Antigone* 86, 94,
   98; drive 52, 57; imprinting 65; libido
   24–5, 52; object 63–4, 66–8, 118; passion
   53; process 26, 52, 62, 65–8, 123;

Index   137

repetitive 29; technical 124; unconscious 75

transgression 79, 93–4, 97–8, 119

transmission 66, 93, 109, 114

Trigg, D. 126n4

truth 26, 42–3, 50–1, 54–6, 61, 68–9, 75, 80, 104–5, 122

Über-Ich 23, 29

uncanny 57, 61, 63–5, 74, 79–86, 88, 90, 94, 98n1–2, 105, 123

unconcealment 42–5, 50, 54–6, 74, 100

unconscious 10, 15–6, 18, 20, 62, 64, 70, 72–3, 75, 100, 113–4, 125, 125n1; caregiving 65; communication 70, 73; creativity 69, 73–5; guilt 123; identification 111; instinct 51; psychical reality 51; receptivity 73–4, 111; suffering 123; thought 15

unheimlich 81, 84

Unheimlichkeit 123

unity 46, 49, 54–5

Vaneigem, R. 33n7, 125n2

Verfügt 98n2

violence 81–6, 88, 90, 93–4, 98, 98n2, 104, 107, 115–6, 119, 121

Virginia Tech 119

war 107–9, 112–4, 18, 120, 126n2

weakness 107

Weber, M. 115

Western Secular Enlightenment 4; *see also* humanism

white supremacy 120

Winnicot 6, 19, 31, 46, 55, 57, 58n1, 61, 63, 66–7, 71–2, 74, 125, 126n5

wish 14–6, 20, 47, 108

word-presentations 4; *see also* *Wortvorstellungen*

Wortvorstellungen 4; *see also* word-presentations

Printed in the United States
by Baker & Taylor Publisher Services